Preview

What if I could share with you a system that would allow you to buy a house, never look at it, and have it sold in less than two hours, all from the comfort of your home?

And what if it was a proven system so easy that you can do it without any cash, credit, or previous experience?

And what if by simply working the system you can buy and sell 1, 3, 5, even 10 houses a month, never qualify for a loan, and make $5,000, $10,000, $25,000, even $50,000 on each transaction?

I know it sounds too good to be true, but I do it every month. And you don't have to take my word for it. Take a look at the quotes and reviews on the back cover of this book from some of the most respected real estate authors and teachers around.

In this book, *Getting Started in Real Estate Day Trading* you will discover the little-known secrets of how you can profit from the current depressed real estate market. I've developed a system that uses the Internet, phone, and fax machines to literally buy and sell houses the same day and never look at a single one of them.

I use the system full time, but I'm also a speaker and real estate educator, and thousands of my students are now using the system to buy and sell houses in the United States, Canada, Australia, New Zealand, China, Japan, Israel, Philippines, Spain, Demark, and elsewhere.

So, if it works in all of these areas, it will work in your city or town.

In this book, you will not only discover exactly how it is done but you will also receive many *free* downloadable forms, documents, and even *free* admission to one of my intensive three-day boot camps where you will get hands-on training—a $2,500 value.

In addition to that, because you bought this book I will give you a free one-on-one strategy session directly with me or with one of my strategists to help you jump-start your Real Estate Day Trading business.

I hope you enjoy this innovative book, and I look forward to helping you get started in Real Estate Day Trading.

Sincerely,
Larry Goins

PS In your free 30-minute one-on-one strategy session, we will show you how to jump-start your day trading business and take these concepts from bookcase to bank account. We want to discover your likes, dislikes, strengths, weaknesses, assets, liabilities, where you are now, where you want to be in your real estate investing career, and most of all how we can help you reach all of your goals.

In Real Estate Day Trading, you don't have to have experience or a college degree. We'll show you exactly what to do in our strategy session with you. To book your free strategy session with one of my start-up specialists or me, go to www.realestatedaytrading.com and click on "free strategy session," or call 877-LarryGoins.

Getting Started in
Real Estate
DAY TRADING

Getting Started in
Real Estate
DAY TRADING

**Proven Techniques for Buying and Selling
Houses the Same Day Using the Internet!**

LARRY GOINS

WILEY

John Wiley & Sons, Inc.

Published by John Wiley & Sons, Inc., Hoboken, New Jersey.
Published simultaneously in Canada.

For general information on our other products and services or for technical support, please contact our Customer Care Department within the United States at (800) 762-2974, outside the United States at (317) 572-3993 or fax (317) 572-4002.

Wiley also publishes its books in a variety of electronic formats. Some content that appears in print may not be available in electronic books. For more information about Wiley products, visit our web site at www.wiley.com.

ISBN 978-0-470-41862-8

Printed in the United States of America.

10 9 8 7 6 5 4 3 2 1

To my wife, Pam,
who is always standing behind me
and believing in me no matter what I do,
to my children Linda and Noah, and in memory of
Lawrence Goins. You taught me so much
about life, and I miss you every day!

CONTENTS

Downloadable Forms

FOREWORD

To me, it is always a stunning act when someone moves from thought to action. Larry Goins has done exactly that. Not just in this book, but in his life. Through his love, commitment, and passion for life, he has deliberately and brilliantly created a new life for himself and those he loves.

And now, through this book, he has created a new life for you.

That's what this book means to me.

Unlike so many how-to-do-it books, *Getting Started in Real Estate Day Trading* literally takes you, the aspirer to a better life, through a step-by-step process to transform the way you relate to the world of money and work. Larry's book will help you create new possibilities that never existed for you before now.

Or did they?

Is it possible that we all can live in this very same world, and yet, no matter how important our lives are, miss the opportunities that are presented to us everywhere we look?

If only we could see!

If only we could see what Larry Goins, and so many others like Larry, can see—that remains invisible to the rest of us.

That's what this book means to me as well. It's an invitation to you to see—the extraordinary through the seemingly ordinary; the potential, immediately, of living a life beyond the ordinary—a life of immense opportunity.

It is that kind of genius that entrepreneurs, such as Larry Goins, Ray Kroc of McDonald's, Michael Dell of Dell Computer, Bill Gates of Microsoft, and so many more create for the rest of us.

Larry's book gives you an opportunity to take a leap beyond your current life, beyond your imagination, beyond your barriers and obstacles, and beyond your limitations.

All you need do is read it. And then, like Larry did after he read my book, do what you read.

Just think. Your future financial independence lies right here in your two hands.

As the great sports company Nike says, "Just do it!"

To your future, to your life.

MICHAEL E. GERBER

Author of *The E-Myth* books and *Awakening the Entrepreneur from Within*

ACKNOWLEDGMENTS

BUSINESS ACKNOWLEDGMENTS

I want to thank my office manager Melanie Bell. You are much more than an office manager. We have been in this together for years, and I look forward to many more years as well. Like you say, "Ain't nothing to it but to do it!" That's why this book is now a reality.

I want to thank my entire Real Estate Day Trading team: Cecelia Lewis, and Matt Lubisich who are in the trenches working this system daily buying and selling houses all over the United States, all from our office in Lake Wylie, South Carolina. You guys are the proof that real estate day trading works and continues to work. You guys make buying and selling houses fun . . . and profitable.

To Kristin Aneralla who every day makes me laugh: You are great at what you do—keeping things running smoothly in the office—and you always do it with a smile.

To Liz Nechio: I have never seen a more organized event coordinator. For that matter, I have never seen a more organized person . . . except for Pam. You are a joy to work with.

To Britt Walker: Britt, you have sent me all around the world to speak at events but the most fun are the fun-filled family vacations that you go on.

To Ryan Smith: You are a great webmaster and programmer and it is great to work with you! Congratulations on purchasing your first foreclosure house at 19 years old!

To Leon Humphrey: Leon you are an inspiration and a great teacher, speaker, coach, real estate day trader, and father and grandfather to your family. I am blessed to know you and work with you.

To Wendy Sweet: No one knows more about real estate finance than you. Not even me. You are a great businessperson and friend.

To Sherry Fredenberg: The original real estate day trader. We miss having you around the office.

To Ki Shin and Brandon Smith, my accountants: You guys rock.

To Michael Gerber: You gave me the inspiration to create a real estate business instead of a job. Without you this book would not have been written.

I also want to thank Richard Narramore at John Wiley & Sons for helping me put this together; Vaughn at Killer Covers who designed a killer cover for the book; Theo Bartek who took my ideas and concepts for this book and organized them in an easy-to-understand manner, making it exciting and easy to read; and Allon Thompson who asked me to get involved in Metrolina Real Estate Investors Association and gave me my first speaking opportunity.

Special thanks to Paul Bauer who has helped me become a much better platform speaker and trainer.

Thanks to all of the many real estate trainers, authors, and speakers I have met and built business relationships and friendships with over the past few years. Thanks to all of the many real estate investor associations, promoters, and other authors and speakers who have invited me to speak at their events. I look forward to working with you for many years to come.

PERSONAL ACKNOWLEDGMENTS

I want to thank my mom Ann Goins Mosteller. You have always believed in me and have never ever told me I couldn't do something. That's why I have always succeeded in everything I have done.

To Lynn Laikin: I have learned so much from you about life and how to be a better dad, husband, and person, and I thank you for that.

To Andy Laikin who is the smartest most successful real estate investor I know: I never make a decision without calling you first. Thanks, Dad.

INTRODUCTION

What if I could show you a brand new, revolutionary way to buy and sell a house and make a minimum of $5,000 in two hours flat? And what if you could do this 10 to 15 times every single month without ever looking at a single house or talking to a realtor, seller, buyer, appraiser, or attorney?

I know it sounds wild, but this is what I do every month. How could it be? It's all because of a tragic life-shattering event that forced me to develop not only a new system of buying and selling real estate, but also a totally new perspective on my role in real estate—or any business for that matter.

I went from *investor* to *business owner.* And that is a very important shift. I went from full-time involvement in every aspect of my business to total absentee ownership. If you hate working every day and never getting ahead, read on, because this could be the answer to your prayers.

I went from working 60-hour weeks for a little money to working a 3-hours-a-month day trading business, where I sell 10 to 15 houses every month making $5,000 to $15,000 on each deal. Yes. You read that right. I did say 3 hours. It isn't a misprint.

I look things over and sign off on deals. I spend about 15 minutes on each deal. I never talk to anybody: no buyers, no sellers, no realtors, and no attorneys. I don't look at houses, and I don't show up for closings. I spend just 15 minutes looking over the paperwork. That's all I do.

How did it happen? I've got to admit up front, that I never thought of doing this myself. I never planned it. I never would have done it voluntarily. But because of unexpected events, I had to do something radical and new that had never been done before. Why? In order to survive.

The traumatic event happened a little over 10 years ago. I was married to a beautiful woman, and we had a two-year-old daughter, Linda. I didn't have a real estate business. I didn't speak at seminars in front of thousands of people all over the country about how to get rich day trading real estate, far from it.

My job as a mortgage broker took an amazing amount of time. I wanted to make more money and spend more time with my family so I decided to get into real estate investing.

But I was terrible at it. I just couldn't make it click. It was all a big hodgepodge to me. I spent too many weekends spinning my wheels with nothing to show for it. With a full-time job, and a new family, real estate investing was just too much work for no money.

But life was good. We had just moved into a house that we had bought the previous year, and my wife was happy as a stay-at-home mom.

Then it happened. My wife found a lump in her breast, and it turned out to be breast cancer. She started going through chemo, radiation, and surgery. She was only 28 years old.

Real estate had to wait. We were now in survival mode. My mother-in-law, who is a nurse, left her job at a hospice in Florida and moved in to take care of my wife and daughter, so I could work to keep the bills paid. She is a saint.

Two and a half years later, in January of 2001, my wife lost her battle with cancer. After helping Linda and me get adjusted, my mother-in-law went back to Florida. There I was, an only parent with a four-year-old daughter who had just lost her mommy.

After a while, I was motivated to try real estate again, but not like before. Previously, I had dabbled in real estate and wasted a lot of time. Now I had even less time because it was just Linda and me. I couldn't afford to dabble anymore. I had to make good things happen because Linda was depending on me—I had my back against a wall, and no matter what I was facing, I had to succeed. You may have been through a similar situation where you had to rise up and take action.

I decided that this time I was going to make it in real estate. I had to find a way to get maximum results in minimum time. I had to do it without working nights and weekends, and I had to do it all while still working a full-time job.

The first thing I did was immerse myself in education.

I attended every course, seminar, and meeting I could find. I studied every real estate course I could get my hands on. I went to the Learning Annex Real Estate and Wealth Expo, and learned from Donald Trump. His teachings about thinking big, finding your passion, going with your gut, and never quitting were priceless. I live by them. Many times Donald Trump's words would echo through my head, "Since you have to think anyway, you might as well think big." "Rich Dad" Robert Kiyosaki made me realize that I had to start thinking like a rich dad thinks. If not for myself, then at least for the sake of my daughter.

It soon became clear to me that I had to come up with my own way of doing real estate. I had to maximize my time and efforts by using technology and applying it to real estate investing. I realized it was now possible to use the Internet, cell phone, e-mail, and fax to buy and sell houses in a fraction of the time most investors spend on their deals. Now I'm a technophobe, but the necessity of raising my daughter and keeping my family together made me go the extra mile to find a way I could deal in real estate part time without working nights or weekends. I had to reserve nights and weekends for family, because they mean everything to me.

The second thing I did was study success and technology in other industries.

I researched Internet marketers, software companies, mortgage companies, franchises, and more. I bought courses, went to seminars, and read lots of books. I read *Business @ the Speed of Thought* (New York: Warner Books, 1999) by Bill Gates; *The E-Myth Revisited: Why Most Businesses Don't Work and What to Do About It* (Cambridge, MA: Ballinger, 1986) by Michael Gerber; *Hyper-Growth: Applying the Success Formula of Today's Fastest Growing Companies* (New York: John Wiley & Sons, 1991) by Skip Weitzen, and many more. I learned how big companies set up systems, so the businesses operate at maximum efficiency, while the leaders take themselves out of the picture.

Michael Gerber's words made an enormous impression on me: "Most people are too busy working *in* their business to work *on* their business. The system is the solution. It works so you don't have to." He taught me how to create a business based on systems and how to become an owner, rather than a manager.

Michael says if you have a business and it can't run without you, then you don't really have a business. What you have is a job. Well, like most people who get into real estate, I already had a job; I didn't need another one. See, most people get into real estate to get *out* of a job they already have. Not to create another one. But most turn real estate into a second job. That wasn't for me and probably not for you either.

I also learned how to structure deals, find value, and become a great negotiator from my father-in-law Andy Laikin. He is the best negotiator and real estate investor I have ever met.

All of that led me to step three. I took action on what I had learned.

I created a system that allowed me to become successful in real estate by working only a few hours a week. That's when real estate day trading was born—out of necessity. The old way simply didn't work for me. Sure I incorporated many of the tried-and-proven strategies. But I went a step beyond, and then many, many more steps beyond, until I arrived at something that was truly new and revolutionary.

Real estate day trading is based on wholesaling properties to investors. But it is much more than wholesaling. It is being able to buy and sell a property anywhere in the United States without ever looking at it and having it sold in two hours and close on the same day. My team and I have taken wholesaling to a much higher level.

Using this real estate day trading system, I am now able to buy and sell 5 to 10 houses every month. But most important, I've learned to take myself out of the process completely by training other people to work for me on a commission basis. Now my company buys up to 15 houses every month. We have bought and sold properties in nine different states, all without ever leaving our office in Lake Wylie, South Carolina.

And as Michael Gerber taught, I've set up my business to operate at maximum efficiency, and I've taken myself out of the picture. That's why I never talk to a single seller or realtor myself, ever.

I have incorporated a lot of technology to automate my business. We do all of our business with phone, fax, e-mail, and the Internet. In deciding what technologies to use, I had two rules: It had to be easy to follow. And it had to bring technology down to a level where anyone, and I mean anyone, could use it without any specialized training whatsoever.

As I mentioned, I'm not a technology buff. Frankly, technology scares me. My dad used to say "if it wasn't for Thomas Edison, we would all be watching TV by candlelight." He was kidding of course, but that's almost the way I look at technology. It's like e-mail. I have no idea how it works. All I know is if I write someone an e-mail and click send, a little while later they reply to me, but I have no idea how it got there or back to me. The good news is I don't need to know how it works. All I need to know is how to use it. But I am able to manage it without having any special training. In fact, I'm not even a college grad.

HOW THIS BOOK WILL HELP YOU

This book includes an easy-to-follow, step-by-step system for you to employ all the labor-saving technologies I have used to put my day trading business on autopilot.

I'm going to show you how to spend a little time upfront setting up your business so you will have lots of time letting your business work for you instead of the other way around. Once you have it set up, it can produce three, four, five, or even ten $5,000+ paydays for you each month.

In *Getting Started in Real Estate Day Trading*, I'm not talking about conventional real estate investing. Investing is where you put thousands of dollars into a property, spend thousands more to fix it up, rent it out, and then hope that it goes up in price so that you can eventually sell it for a profit.

What I'm talking about is buying a house at 10:00 AM, selling it at 10:30 AM to a buyer/investor and pocketing a quick $5,000 to $15,000 profit in one day, and then doing the same thing over and over again many times every month. This is what it means to do real estate as a business, rather than investing in real estate.

You'll have no money invested. So your money is not at risk. You'll have your buyer lined up ahead of time to buy the property for you as soon as you buy it from your seller. It's easy to do, if you know how. This is all my company does.

If you're a veteran at real estate investing, this book can give you a new way to think about what you do. I recently got an e-mail from a student who told me he has been investing 16 years. After looking at my system and starting to set up his own day trading system, he came to the realization that even though he has been investing 16 years, someone brand new with no experience can get in the business and literally dominate the market by simply using the day trading system.

He told me that the way I teach my students to buy houses levels the playing field. You don't have to worry anymore about experienced investors taking your deals. You can actually get a jump on them.

The guy that said he has been investing for 16 years . . . Well, is that 16 years of experience or a single year of experience repeated 16 times? We have all heard, "if you keep on doing what you always do, you keep on getting what you have always gotten." It's the same thing.

In this book, I'll show you exactly what I do. I teach you how to set up a real estate day trading business, operate your business, and automate it. I don't leave anything out.

By the way, my story turned out to be a happy one. I got remarried. My daughter Linda is now 12 years old, and I have a son Noah who is 4 years old. I met my wife Pam online. I figured if I could find a house online, then I could find a spouse online. In fact, here is a recent picture of our family on a Disney cruise with the grandparents. I actually had a deal close while we were on this cruise. Now that's real estate day trading.

From left to right: Andy, Lynn, Ann, Linda, Pam, Me, Noah

SECTION I

REAL ESTATE DAY TRADING: A NEW WAY TO MAKE BIG MONEY BUYING AND SELLING HOUSES THE SAME DAY

CHAPTER 1

CLICK A MOUSE, SELL A HOUSE: REAL ESTATE DAY TRADING IS THE EASIEST AND FASTEST WAY TO MAKE $90,000 A YEAR (OR MORE) WHILE KEEPING YOUR JOB ... IF YOU WANT TO

Forget all the stories you have heard about real estate being difficult and risky. Technology-based real estate day trading is a whole new way to do real estate, which is only possible because of the Internet, fax, e-mail, cell phones, digital cameras, and other new technologies. I can look online and see dozens of pictures of houses for sale in my nearby city of Charlotte, North Carolina, or all the way up in Medford, Oregon. I've actually day traded houses in more than nine states so far over the Internet without even seeing the house or leaving my office. So far my team has bought and sold houses in North Carolina, South Carolina, Florida, Ohio, Pennsylvania, Illinois, Michigan, Georgia, Texas and Tennessee.

I communicate with buyers and sellers using my web site. They use my web site to get information, apply for funding, and view pictures of my houses. The web site also contains contracts and full instructions so that they can make offers without me being involved. I call the web site my "Ultimate Internet Marketing Machine." I've set up my web site to send out e-mails from me automatically to keep in touch with my buyers and sellers. I use my web site to interact with attorneys, contractors, appraisers, title companies, and home inspectors in many locations who do my closings for me. You can check out my site at www.InvestorsRehab.com and get on my buyer list or submit a property to me there as well.

I use the Internet and e-mail for social networking with investors, online user groups, and online classifieds. Google and eBay play a pivotal role in my real estate day trading business. The way I do real estate it's almost like virtual real estate—no more driving from house to house; rehabbing; or dealing with mortgages, taxes, insurance, or tenants. Just a clean buy-sell transaction in one day with a quick $5,000 or more paycheck. And no bricks-and-mortar encumbrances to deal with afterward. It's a lot like day trading stocks. You're in and out by the end of the day. And you are $5,000 or more richer.

But actually, "I" do none of it. For when I use the word "I," I mean we; I mean my company and my system. I am *personally* only a very small part of my real estate day trading system. It is actually *my system* that does all these things for me.

REAL ESTATE DAY TRADING MAKES FAILURE A THING OF THE PAST

The biggest reason people fail in real estate is because they are alone. At work there are other people around, and you don't have to do everything by yourself. But in real estate it's different.

When people start out in real estate, they have a high level of excitement. They hear stories about the success many people are having in real estate. These stories make it all sound so easy. Uncle Harry comes for Thanksgiving dinner and brags about how much money he's making in real estate.

With a head full of success stories, neophytes plunge in. But it doesn't take long before reality sets in. Soon they get hung up on all the boring details and get frustrated by all the mind-boggling unknowns that haunt their every move. Their enthusiasm starts to cool.

Finally it's too much to bear. Their confidence wanes, and their resolve is broken. They can no longer muster the powerful enthusiasm they need to succeed in this game. They conclude that real estate is just too difficult and risky.

SMALL PROBLEMS APPEAR LARGE THROUGH NOVICE EYES

Actually, it only seems that way because novice real estate investors lack knowledge. Everything looks daunting at first. Problems like making offers, that are nothing to a real estate veteran, seem insurmountable to the novice.

Most novices find it hard to make offers on houses. Their heads are filled with doubts and fears. They wonder if they are making a mistake and offering too much. They're afraid the seller or realtor will see through them or not believe they are for real. They are afraid their offer will be rejected, and they are even more afraid that their offer will be accepted. The biggest fear is getting stuck with a house they paid too much for and/or will never be able to sell.

To the experienced real estate day trader, making offers is just a routine task they do every day. They know exactly what to do, what to say, and how much to offer. It's no big deal. I make 10 or more offers to buy houses every single day. Later in this book, I'll explain how I can do this with complete confidence, safety, and zero risk.

Finding a buyer is another big problem to most novices. They are so afraid nobody will ever buy their house. The truth is the exact opposite. Buyers are desperate to find good houses to invest in. Later, I'll show you how to find the kind of houses that buyers desperately want to buy and how to buy them at steep discounts. Then buyers will line up to buy houses from you.

To me, buyers are never a problem. As you'll see, I have buyers fighting to buy houses from me. They even send me deposit checks in advance for houses I haven't even bought yet. That's how motivated my buyers are.

Closings are also a big bugaboo for most beginners. It seems so intimidating to close a real estate deal. With all the formidable paperwork and formalities it does seem daunting. But it's really not.

Once you've been through it a few times, it's a piece of cake. More important, once you have a few competent professionals on your team, an attorney or title company, you don't need to be involved in closings. Let your professionals handle all the details. That's their job, and they're much better at it than you or me, anyway.

Funding is also a big problem in most peoples' minds. But when you're day trading, you don't really have to know about mortgages, bankers, brokers, or underwriters. You don't need long-term debt because you're not investing in the house long term. I close many of my deals without any money at all out of my pocket, except for a small deposit or option fee.

If you need some funds to close, as I'll explain, it's easy to use your own lines of credit or find private day funders to let you use some of their money to close a deal. They give you the money in the morning, and they get it back in the evening, with a fee. It's a no-brainer. I do it all the time. Later, I'll show you how.

Another big mistake that beginners make is getting involved in complicated forms of real estate investing. They have heard about somebody making big money in luxury houses. So they start chasing luxury houses. They soon discover how treacherous it is and find themselves in way over their heads. The luxury house market is tricky and best left to experienced investors. It's not a good place for beginners to start.

Some people get enamored with multifamily houses, apartments, or commercial real estate. Sure, many real estate moguls have built fortunes in these markets. But it's much too complex for someone who's just starting out part time.

Another problem is delayed gratification. It took Donald Trump about three years to complete his first commercial deal buying a huge property on New York's west side from the bankrupt Penn Central Railroad. Donald Trump had the guts and years of previous experience to see him through. But most of us are not Donald Trump. Especially in the beginning, we need to see some tangible results a lot faster than that.

Even investing in fixer-uppers to rehab and rent is a long complicated process fraught with dangers that can take up to a year or more to complete and sell. There's a lot to know, a lot to understand, and a lot of pitfalls and surprises that could haunt you along the way. Real estate day trading is nothing like this. It's fast, there's no financial risk, and it's simple and uncomplicated. It's find it, flip it, and forget it.

REAL ESTATE DAY TRADING IS A CONFIDENCE BUILDER

With real estate day trading, you're in and out in one day, with no risk and no unpleasant surprises. You don't need to know as much. It's also less time-consuming to do. You can do it all using the Internet, e-mail, phone, and fax. You don't have to look at properties because it's all done by the numbers.

You have no tenants, mortgages, maintenance, taxes, or insurance. You don't have to worry about tenants not paying, destroying your property, or frantic phone calls in the middle of the night.

As I'll show you, real estate day trading is the simplest and least complicated form of real estate there is. It's the kind of real estate business that you can systematize and bring in others to run for you. That's exactly what I have done. I'll show you how to do this, too.

It's a perfect business for beginners who just want to do real estate part time while they keep their jobs. You can use this system for part-time income, as a business to build your wealth, or just to buy a house to live in at below market prices.

Real estate day trading is a real confidence builder because you get small victories fast. After you read this book, you'll be able to do your first deal in 90 days or less. I've hired people with no experience and trained them to day trade houses for my company. Using my system, some were able to close their first deal in as soon as five weeks. Follow the directions in this book, and you'll be able to do the same thing.

MAKE $90,000 A YEAR (OR MORE) WHILE KEEPING YOUR PRESENT JOB

I'll show you how to find houses that you can make money on and explain how to make offers on them. I'll show you how to find lots of motivated buyers who will immediately buy houses from you. I'll teach you how to make $5,000 or more on each deal. I'll show you how to turn this whole process into something that you can systematize and automate. After that, it's just a numbers game. The more offers you make, the more money you'll make. It's that simple.

Let's look at the numbers. If you make 10 offers a week every single week, you'll be making 40 offers a month. Of the 40 offers you make, you should be able to sign about six contracts every month. Some months it will be more, some months it will be less. But six contracts is a reliable estimate, if you make 40 offers. That's six potential deals and six potential $5,000 paydays.

But not all of these deals will close. Don't worry too much about any one deal. Remember, it's just a numbers game. If you get six deals a month, you'll probably close one to two deals a month, maybe more.

These numbers are based on the actual results we get in our office. My people are making 5 to 10 offers a day every day and closing 10 to 15 deals every month. This is what it takes. If you make 40 offers a month, you'll close one to two deals.

That averages out to roughly one and a half deals per month. If you close one and a half deals a month, you'll make $90,000 a year. And that is assuming you only make the minimum of $5,000 on each deal, so it could be a lot more.

It's not hard to make 10 offers a week. You can make one offer a night and five on Saturday. How much time do you think that would take? Not very much, especially if you use my streamlined system to enable you to work smarter rather than harder.

The key, as I mentioned before, is to do the most productive work in the shortest amount of time. In the following chapters, I'll teach you how to get part-time helpers, answering services, call capture services, autoresponders, and many other time savers to reduce the amount of time you have to spend on nonessential tasks. This will free you to concentrate your time on doing the one job that is most important: making offers.

Now that you know what to do, set your goals, and don't let anyone or anything stop you. As Donald Trump says, "Never, ever give up!" Just commit to making 10 offers a week, and you'll make at least $7,500 a month. That's a nice part-time income. At the end of one year, you'll be $90,000 (or more) richer. Let's go for it!

CHAPTER 2

REAL ESTATE DAY TRADING: A BUSINESS DONE ENTIRELY BY PHONE, FAX, E-MAIL, AND INTERNET

I like to make a little bit on a lot of properties. I call it "Stack 'em deep and sell 'em cheap." Day trading real estate is a strategy based on *wholesaling* property to other investors who are ready, willing, and able to buy from you at the right price so that they can make money on the property, too.

TIME LINE FOR A TYPICAL DEAL

Day trading means that you buy and sell a house the same day. However, just as in day trading stocks, you have to do due diligence, research, and preparation before the big day when you close on the property and resell it a few minutes or hours later. Typically the whole process leading up to a *day trade* takes about 30 days. During that period, you locate a house you can make a big profit on that you want to buy. You negotiate with the seller and make a deal. Then you have 15 days for due diligence, title search, inspection, and appraisal. Then 15 more days to find a buyer before your big *double closing*.

THE 10-STEP DAY TRADING PROCESS

Building a fully functioning day trading system is a 10-step process. You go from zero money and experience, to a fully automated system to generate

9

1, 3, 5, 10, or more automatic $5,000+ paydays a month. But it won't happen overnight. First you have to build your system, then you work the system to generate money, then you completely automate and delegate all the parts of the system.

Step 1. Define Your Target Properties

Most novices spend too much time looking at properties that don't stand a chance of making money. In Chapter 3, I'm going to make it crystal clear exactly what kinds of houses you should target. You'll learn the sizes, types, and price ranges of these houses. And I'll warn you about the kinds of houses to keep away from. You can then approach the market with the confidence of knowing what you are looking for—what kinds of properties in what price ranges, locations, and conditions.

Step 2. Separate Good Deals from Bad Deals

Many beginners make deals by the seat of their pants. They are so eager to get started that they just jump in without knowing what they are doing. I call it the "I gotta get a deal" syndrome, which I will explain in Chapter 15.

Others recognize the dangers, get scared, procrastinate, and put off making offers. They're so afraid of failure that they stay safe by doing nothing. Or they spend so much time deliberating on each deal that by the time they make up their minds, it's too late and the deal has passed them by. Just remember, "You can't steal in slow motion." Now I don't literally mean *steal,* but be aware that if you can't make a fast decision, the deal will be gone before you know it.

Many real estate investors are slow to act because of the fear of rejection or fear of having their offers turned down. So they are tentative and timid during negotiations. As a result, sellers and buyers don't believe them because they don't talk or act with conviction.

In real estate day trading, you need to make fast, confident offers that carry weight with your sellers. That way you can stand out from the crowd and be respected as someone who can follow through—someone who can make offers and close deals. In Chapter 4, I'll teach you my secret formula for making lots of offers quickly and safely—my instant property analysis. Using this technique, you'll be able to make offers on houses during the first phone call with sellers, safely and with confidence.

Step 3. Build a Database of Motivated Buyers

In day trading, you need to close fast. Therefore, you need motivated buyers in place before you start. That way, when you have a house to sell, all you need to do is announce it and let them come to you with contracts. Once you've established a database of buyers, you don't have to chase buyers. When you have something to sell, they come to you.

You don't have time to scramble around looking for buyers at the last minute. You need a database of motivated buyers who are ready, willing, and prequalified to buy houses from you.

In Chapter 5, you'll learn how to use the latest Internet technology and Web 2.0 technology to create an online database of motivated buyers. You'll learn how to use the latest strategies in online marketing, social networking, and online prospecting. And I promise that no matter what computer skill you are lacking, you can do it. I've also included some of the most powerful offline methods of finding buyers as well.

Step 4. Create an Influx of Motivated Sellers

The next step, explained in Chapter 6, is to create a swarm of motivated sellers who want to sell their houses to you at sharply discounted prices. You'll learn dozens of online and offline methods to find distressed sellers. Most important, I'll teach you how to automate this whole process so that once it's up and running all you need to do is keep it going regardless of what the market conditions are. This guarantees you a steady flow of houses on which to get contracts and offer to the folks in your motivated buyers database.

Step 5. Put a Reliable Source of Funding in Place

As a real estate day trader, there are many ways to close deals with no money or credit. But many times, you'll need to fund a deal for 24 hours. I'm not talking about investing money in the traditional sense, where money is tied up for many months or even years. What I'm talking about is what I call *day funding*—the overnight borrowing of enough money to close the deal.

In Chapter 7 you'll learn how to access some of the cheapest money on the planet. You'll be surprised at how much money you can raise quickly online. And you'll learn how to find private investors or *day funders* who will fund one-day deals for a small fee. Remember, you need to do this before you close on any deal. In fact, you should make sure your funding is in place before you make your first offer. Chapter 7 explains how.

Step 6. Build Your Dream Team of Trained Professionals

To streamline your system and sell houses fast, you need trained professionals as part of your day trading system. Chapter 8 tells you how to use the Internet and social networking to find the right professionals to add to your dream team and how to screen them for competence, efficiency, and reliability.

Step 7. Prepare Your Buying and Selling Contracts

In Chapter 9, you'll learn all about the paperwork necessary to buy and sell properties in one day. The contracts are simple, but the clauses are important. You'll learn about three super-important "must have" clauses that you need in your contracts to protect yourself. Without these clauses, real estate day trading will not work. Be sure to prepare all your contracts before you start day trading. It's not that hard to do. But it's a very important step.

Step 8. Start Day Trading

Now you're ready to make money. When you reach this step, your system is complete, and you can start day trading and start making those $5,000 plus paydays. In Chapter 10, you'll learn how to make offers and negotiate deals. You'll learn what to say to realtors and what to say to owners/sellers. In Chapter 11, you'll learn how to verify and certify your deal by getting a title search, a contractor repair estimate, and an appraisal. In Chapter 12, you'll learn how to advertise your house to motivated buyers in your database. And in Chapter 13, you'll learn the procedure for closing the deal with the assistance of your real estate attorney or title company.

Step 9. Use Advanced Techniques to Create a Buying Frenzy

Once you are an experienced real estate day trader, you can start implementing advanced techniques to start a buying frenzy among your buyers. It all has to do with a whisper campaign and a short list of supermotivated prequalified buyers. Think about this: I don't have to sell my houses anymore because I have buyers lined up to buy them. Do you see the difference?

Using these techniques, I have buyers begging me to sell them my houses. I'll share all of my secrets with you in Chapter 12.

Step 10. Take Yourself Out of the Loop

In Chapter 14, you'll find out how to automate and delegate 92 percent of the work, leaving you almost completely out of the day-to-day buying and selling. Everyone else does the work. But you maintain complete control and must approve every deal. You will learn how to use virtual assistants for routine tasks and commission-based property acquisition managers to make offers, negotiate deals, and sell houses for you.

After completing this step, you will have a business that's based on a *system,* not on *you.* Once it's fully implemented, you will no longer be needed in the day-to-day operations. Yet you will still buy and sell 10 or more houses every month. That will be the fulfillment of what Michael Gerber defined as an *E-Myth* company, applied to real estate.

So there you have it, the whole plan.

You need to line up your motivated buyers, funding, contracts, team of professionals, and system for finding motivated sellers in advance. You need to know how to approach buyers, sellers, private investors, and professionals who work with you—what you say and how you are going to gain their trust and confidence. You need a good follow-up system to keep in touch with your buyers, sellers, and success team.

Once you have all the pieces in place, you'll be able to go out and make offers with power and confidence. After you do this for a while your reputation will grow, and good deals will start coming to you.

WHAT YOU NEED TO GET STARTED

You need very little to start a real estate day trading business. You don't need an elaborate office full of paid staff. All you need is a computer, fax, printer, Internet access, and a telephone.

You'll also need the following services: answering service, autoresponder, web browser with tabbed browsing, database software for follow-up e-mail and data files, and a web site.

And you need to allocate time to set up your day trading system—about two hours a day for 30 days and you should have everything in place. After that, it takes about 10 hours a week to find motivated sellers and make 10 offers.

Remember, it's a numbers game: If you make 10 offers a week, 40 a month, you should close about one to two deals per month, and make $5,000 a deal. These are conservative estimates. You might actually do a lot better.

After you have it up and running for a while, you can hire virtual assistants to do all the online searching for you and bring you the names of motivated sellers that fit your criteria. Then you'll only need to spend about two hours a week making offers, and you'll still close one to two deals a month and make $5,000 to $10,000 a month. If you want to make more money, then simply make more offers.

Then, when you're ready, you can use commissioned property acquisition managers to triple those numbers without any additional hours of work. Then we're talking three to six deals a month, and $15,000 to $30,000 in income. And you'll be completely out of the loop. Is this business exciting or what!

But remember, these numbers are extremely conservative. In calculating the money you'll make, I talked about a $5,000 payday. But in actuality, my paydays are often much larger than that. I usually make a minimum of 5 percent and many times 10 percent per deal. For example, if you sell a house with a $50,000 "after-repaired" value, you'll make $5,000. But if you sell a house with a $100,000 after-repaired value, you'll get $10,000 on the deal. The higher the after-repaired value, the more money you should make. So your monthly income could be much greater than the $15,000 to $30,000 shown in the previous paragraph!

Of course, you've got to put out some effort to make this work. And I know this might be a little uncomfortable at first. But let me let you in on a little secret. There is no growth in the comfort zone! Every level of income requires a different you. I am not the same person I was when I first got started, and neither will you be after you learn and implement these strategies.

Do you think it's an accident that you're reading this book today? I think everything happens for a reason. I can't tell you how many calls and e-mails I get from excited students telling me they have been hoping and praying for something like this. See your mind and your money go together. Your money is a reflection of your mind.

Now let's get started building your real estate day trading system!

SECTION II

Set Up Your Own Day Trading Money System and Start Making $5,000 to $10,000 Cash Paydays in 30 Days

CHAPTER 3

IT'S EASIER TO FIND A HOUSE FOR A BUYER THAN A BUYER FOR A HOUSE: GET INVESTORS LINED UP TO BUY (WHOLESALE) FROM YOU

If you've been watching TV lately, you might wonder how in the heck I can say that you'll have buyers lined up to buy from you. It seems farfetched or even impossible given the state of the real estate markets as I write this. Selling a house at full price on the retail market is difficult and time-consuming.

You have to show it over and over to people who seem interested but you never hear from again. You wait and wait and wait for someone to make an offer. Then you get an offer and have to go through the agony of a negotiation, followed by an inspection, and then an appraisal. Then if you finally get a signed contract, you've got to wait until the buyer can find financing. This whole process is complicated, time-consuming, and unpleasant. It's no way to make money. It is hard to sell houses for full retail value in the buyers' market that we have now.

But, as a real estate day trader, I do none of that. Yet I have buyers lined up to buy from me. I send out a simple e-mail, and within a few hours or less, I get multiple offers. I pick one and keep the others as backups in case my first buyer falls through for some reason. A lot of realtors have deals fall through at the last minute because of financing, inspection, and so on, and

17

then they have to put the property back on the market. When that happens to me, I already have a backup offer ready to go. Is this great or what?

Why is it so easy? It's easy because I have highly motivated buyers who are hungry for the houses I sell.

IT'S ALL ABOUT FINDING HOUSES FOR BUYERS

Most people think about finding buyers for their houses. I think about house selling in a whole different way. I think about finding houses for my buyers. I concentrate on finding houses to sell to investors at wholesale prices. My buyers only buy wholesale. They never pay full retail price.

These investors rehab the house and then sell it to homeowners who will get a conventional loan, live in it, maintain it, and pay the mortgage, taxes, and insurance. Or they will rent it or lease option it to people who will live in it and pay enough rent for the investor to cover all expenses and make a positive cash flow. These are good ways to make money in traditional real estate investing, and many people do it—I used to use these methods myself. But these strategies are much more time-consuming and costly than the day trading that I do. Using the day trading system is the fastest way to quick cash.

REAL ESTATE DAY TRADING VERSUS REAL ESTATE INVESTMENT

Real estate day trading is a real estate business, not an investment. I don't invest my money, and I don't risk my money in residential real estate. Instead, I provide a service—providing properties to investors at wholesale prices—and I get paid a fee for my service, like any other service provider. When I want to invest my money long term, I invest in triple net lease commercial properties or use my money to become a day funder or hard money lender to other investors and/or rehabbers.

My buyers, on the other hand, are real estate investors. They invest their money buying the property and making the repairs necessary to bring a house to excellent condition in order to sell it retail or lease it to end user consumers. I'm in the real estate business, and they're real estate investors.

It's just like a manufacturing business. The manufacturer produces the product and sells wholesale to stores that retail to the public. In this case, I don't make the product, but I find products (houses) that retailers (investors) fix up and sell or rent to the public (the homeowner or renter). Investors make profits from renting or selling the product (houses) retail.

Investors/buyers are very motivated. They are hungry for more and more product (houses) to fix up and sell. They've got to have a lot of houses in the pipeline in order to make a profit. The more houses they buy and fix up, the more profit they make.

Homeowners buy houses to live in. They only buy a few houses throughout their lives and are very particular about what they buy. It's a very personal thing. The house has to be right for them. And everything has to be in tip-top condition. They take a long time making up their minds on a house. They need to fall in love with it before they buy it.

It's not so with investors. Investors never think of houses in terms of whether they would live there themselves. To investors, a house is just a product to retail to end users. Their decision is completely impersonal and by the numbers. They will buy a house quickly if it's the type of house they can fix up and sell fast and if they can buy it at a low price. If you give these investors/buyers what they want, they will buy.

THINK LIKE A SUPPLIER

You don't have to waltz real estate investors around a property and do a song and dance to get them to buy. You don't have to dress up the property. You don't have to tell them how nice the neighbors are or how great the school system is.

But they don't buy just any house, at any price, in just any location. They have many definite needs in a house. If you bring them houses that fit their needs, you won't have to work hard to find them. They'll beat a path to your door. And once you have a buyer, you can sell houses to that same buyer many times over. I have one investor/buyer who has bought over 20 houses from me.

But first, you need to learn what they need. If you can supply them with what they need, you'll become very rich and successful. And you won't have to work very hard. The trick is that you've got to think like a supplier.

WHAT KINDS OF HOUSES DO THEY BUY?

The vast majority of investors/buyers are looking for what I call bread-and-butter houses. You should focus on modest houses located in low to middle income areas that are in need of repair.

It's as simple as that. Yet most real estate beginners go wrong by making things too complicated. They have no strategy for choosing where and what to buy and how much to pay. They often end up buying houses they can't possibly make money on, get disappointed, and quit.

Just stick with modest low- to median-priced houses in need of repair. Investors don't necessarily want to repair houses. They just want to make a profit. Houses in need of repair are the most profitable because they are the easiest houses to buy dirt cheap. Investors want these houses so that they can build what's called "sweat equity." They sell the house for a higher value than the cost of repairs.

For your investors/buyers to make a profit, they need houses they can buy dirt cheap. They've got to be cheap enough that you can collect a sizable fee and still sell it to your buyer at a low wholesale price. So, you have to be able to buy the house below wholesale.

The reason to focus on low-priced houses is this. Most of your investors/buyers want low-priced houses that they can easily afford to buy with cash, without the hassle of financing or the need to get a hard money loan or a private money loan (more about that later). When you get into higher-priced houses, you lose a lot of buyers because they don't have enough cash to buy houses with those kinds of price tags or they are scared to take on such a big mortgage.

Using traditional mortgages to buy investment houses is not an option. It's too slow, and it's too hard for most investors to qualify. Banks don't like to lend money on fixer-uppers. Later, I will show you how to get the money you need and how to help your investors/buyers get all the money they need as well, which makes it easier for them to buy from you.

You are not going to find many low-priced houses in need of repair in upscale neighborhoods. There may be some. But they are few and far between. Even if you find a $300,000 home in need of repair in a nice neighborhood, it will be harder to sell to your investors/buyers because very few of them will have that kind of cash to buy a house from you at a moment's notice. As real estate day traders, we want to deal only with buyers who can close fast.

The $300,000 I used in this example is much higher than the median-priced home in my area. If you live in an area like Orange County, California, $300,000 would be below the median for that area.

It's true that some investors make great money on upscale houses. But that's not real estate day trading. Real estate day trading is when you focus on low- to middle-income houses that are in need of repairs. If you do so, you'll find 10 times as many hungry investors who will buy properties (as is, sight unseen) from you. Give them these houses, and you will have buyers who will come back to you over and over again to buy more houses. It's a great repeat business.

LOW INCOME DOESN'T MEAN NO INCOME

Let me be completely clear. I'm talking about clean, safe low- to middle-income areas; places where people work and raise families; where people want and can afford to live. I'm not talking about what I call "war zones." War zones are high-crime areas where many of the inhabitants don't work. These are unsafe areas where crime is rampant and property values are extremely low.

MOST HOUSES ARE NOT FOR YOU

You can ignore most of the houses on the market. Most of these houses are being sold by realtors and homeowners who want to sell their houses retail for full market price. They want to sell, but they don't need to sell. There's a big difference. People who merely want to sell are not motivated enough to sell to you at below retail prices. You don't want to pay any attention to the majority of houses listed at full retail prices. We do buy a lot of properties from realtors, but most of them are bank-owned properties. Think about it. Banks are in the lending business not the real estate business. There is no chance of a bank taking a property off the market because it decided not to sell it. Banks *are* going to sell it eventually, and the sooner the better for the bank.

Buying houses in low- to middle-income areas, that are in need of repair, at below wholesale prices, eliminates most of the houses on the market. It's important to be absolutely clear on this. A good rule of thumb I learned a long time ago is, if there are people jogging in the neighborhood, then the area is probably a little too nice to focus on. The next chapter tells you exactly how to find the houses priced to meet your standards—that can satisfy your buyers and will give you a hefty fee.

In South Carolina where I live, these low-income houses usually sell from $60,000 to $100,000 retail. In your area, that number may be the same or it may be higher. You should just target houses that sell right at or below the median price for existing single-family homes in your area.

GOLDILOCKS HOUSES—NOT TOO BIG, NOT TOO SMALL, JUST RIGHT

Most of your buyers will be looking for houses that are not too big and not too small. Big houses are more expensive. Fewer buyers will be able to come up with the cash to buy them, even if they are located in low-income neighborhoods. The ideal house to sell to investors/buyers has three bed-rooms, two baths, and is typically less than 1,500 square feet. These are what I call "Goldilocks" houses.

You can vary this somewhat. Three-bedroom, one-bath houses are okay, if they are large enough—at least 850 square feet. Four-bedroom, two-bath houses are also good. Don't buy anything smaller than 750 square feet. Home buyers don't want them, realtors don't want them, and your investors/buyers know this and will not buy them from you. Also, many lenders have guidelines that will not allow them to make a loan on a house with less than 750 square feet.

You might consider buying a large two-bedroom house that has enough space to add a third bedroom within the existing square footage. Your investors might be able to make money on that. But you will have to get it for a very low price to afford the cost of constructing a third bedroom. Make sure you can add the third bedroom within the existing square footage. It is much cheaper to do that than add square footage.

One of my students came to me with a two-bedroom, one-bath house that he could pick up very cheap. He wanted to fix it up and sell it retail. It was a great deal, but I advised him not to buy it. When he asked why, I told him that he would never be able to sell that house. Nobody would buy it because almost anyone that can qualify for a home mortgage would not want a two-bedroom house. Most qualified home buyers are looking for houses with at least three bedrooms.

Of course, there are exceptions to every rule. Some home buyers may want to buy and live in a two bedroom. But you drastically reduce the number of retail buyers who may want the property if it is a two bedroom. I always believe in going for the low-hanging fruit first. That's why I stick with three bedroom houses. My buyers/investors favor them.

AVOID TOWNHOUSES AND CONDOS, MULTIFAMILY HOUSES, AND VA/FHA-OWNED HOUSES

To make the most money in real estate day trading you've got to grab the low hanging fruit. I always go for the big numbers. The biggest money and the easiest deals are in low- to middle-income houses—not too big, not too small—that need repairs. Ignore the rest. This includes multifamily houses like duplexes, triplexes, or quads. People who can qualify for mortgages on those don't want to live in them.

Some people buy VA and FHA-owned houses. But I don't typically look at them. There might be some good deals there, but they are very hard to get to. These agencies are hard to negotiate with. It takes a long time to get them to come down in price.

Also I would stay away from townhouses and condos. They are more difficult to rent out with a positive cash flow because of the association fees that have to be paid monthly. Also, they don't hold their value as well and are more susceptible to market corrections.

Your investors/buyers want to buy detached single-family houses, not too big or too small, that need repairs, located in low- to middle-income areas. That should be your focus and your only focus in day trading. That's how you can get them lining up to buy houses from you.

CHAPTER 4

INSTANT PROPERTY ANALYSIS TO IDENTIFY PROFITABLE DEALS

You know that your target houses are located in low- to middle-income neighborhoods. You also know that most of them will be bread-and-butter houses—three-bedroom, two-bath houses in need of repair that you can buy at a big discount. As mentioned before, houses with one bathroom or one and a half bath are okay, too.

Now I'm going to narrow down your search even further. In this chapter, you'll learn how to evaluate houses instantly and make strong offers that will ensure it's a deal where you and your investor/buyer will make money and you'll be able to sell quickly.

The structure of my instant property analysis system works anywhere. But the actual numbers will vary from location to location. Where I live, the cost of houses is on the low side. In Charlotte, North Carolina, and surrounding areas, the houses I buy usually have an "after-repair" value in the $60,000 to $100,000 range. In big cities like New York, Chicago, Los Angeles, Atlanta, Boston, Philadelphia, and San Francisco, the average will be higher. In some of these areas, low-income houses will sell for more than $200,000.

MORE OFFERS MEAN MORE MONEY

In real estate day trading, the more offers you make, the more money you make. Always remember that. Offers are like money in the bank. If you are timid about making offers, you'll never make money in real estate day trading. It's okay if you are timid now but once you start making offers, it will eventually come naturally.

Some people are frightened to make offers on houses being sold "as is." First of all, you don't really know for sure exactly what you're buying, the cost of repairs, how much you can sell the house for, or even if you'll be able to sell it at all. The biggest reason most people don't want to make offers is because their biggest fear is "What do I do if they take it?" In the next chapter, I will show you how to build a database of hungry buyers so you'll never be afraid that your offer will be accepted.

I designed my real estate day trading system to enable you to fearlessly make strong, powerful offers on the first phone call. This chapter explains how to make lots of offers, as many as 10 or 15 a day, without the slightest hesitation.

The first step is *instant property analysis*, which allows you to analyze a house on the first phone call with a seller or a realtor.

Some investors talk to sellers and, after the call is over, spend hours inputting numbers into spreadsheet programs that include every conceivable expense that could ever occur so that the program can spit out return on investment (ROI) numbers for 5 to 10 years into the future. They do all of this to make a simple offer on a small house. By then, they have lost touch with the seller and end up playing phone tag for days or weeks. When they finally get a second phone call with the seller, the moment has passed, and the deal is gone. Using this method it's hard to make very many offers, and it's hard to make any money. It also wastes a lot of time.

In my experience, all you need are a few numbers and a few simple calculations to know exactly what you can offer on any house. In fact, I tell everyone I do business with—investors, realtors, and owners/sellers—that I will make an offer on the phone on any house on the first phone call. I don't hang up until I make an offer.

Remember, making an offer is only the first step toward making a deal. You don't have an actual deal until you go through the negotiation process and reach a meeting of the minds with your sellers.

Making more good offers means making more good deals. It's important to make only good deals. There are many good deals out there to be made. You don't have to waste your time chasing after bad deals that are impossible to make money on. Before making an offer, you've got to know beyond a shadow of a doubt that you will make a lot of money. If not, then just pass. Get off the phone and go on to the next phone call. You don't have to chase bad deals and hope they will magically become good.

This is especially true for beginners. On your first few deals, you want to make sure there is plenty of profit in each deal. In other words, you want your first few deals to be home runs! The worst thing you can do is get involved in a marginal deal and get discouraged and quit the business.

I want you to use my instant property analysis technique to make offers on your first phone call. At first it will feel odd making offers without seeing the property. But after you do it a few times, it will come naturally. The goal is to get your offer to them right away to start the negotiation process.

After all, you are not going to buy the house on the first phone call. The purpose of the first offer is to start the negotiation process and get the seller to feel "attached" to you. When you make an offer, the seller will remember you. You are probably the only person they've talked to who's actually made an offer. You'll impress them as different, and they'll respect you as a doer, rather than just another talker.

My father-in-law, Andy Laikin, is the best real estate investor and negotiator I have ever met. I have learned more from him than from all of the real estate gurus put together. He calls this technique "getting them in the glue." Do this 10 times a day everyday, and you'll create a tremendous momentum that will lead to lots of $5,000 or more paydays! Even if you work part time, and make 10 to 12 offers a week, you could easily close two to four deals a month at $5,000 a deal. Not bad money for a few hours a week.

TWO SIMPLE QUESTIONS

When talking to sellers you need the answers to two simple questions to do my instant property analysis:

1. What will it sell for after it's repaired?
2. How much will it cost to repair?

If it's a rental property you will also need to know the estimated monthly rent. And if it's a for sale by owner (FSBO) property, you need to know the current loan balance and if they are behind on the mortgage payments. That's all you need to know. You already have all the other information, price range, location, number of bedrooms and baths, or you wouldn't be talking to the seller.

What Will It Sell For after It's Repaired?

This is an estimate of how much the house would sell for in good condition. It's based on the price that similar houses in excellent condition have sold for in the same neighborhood. Most realtors who list properties know this information. After they agree to list the property, they always do a competitive market analysis (CMA) for every seller and base the asking price on it. They know how much houses of this size and type are selling for in the area. So don't be afraid to ask them. If the property being listed is a bank-owned property that has been foreclosed on, then the realtor has probably already performed broker price opinion (BPO) on the property to give the bank an idea of the price for which the property should be listed.

And most homeowners know approximately how much their house is worth. Sometimes, a family member or friend happens to be a realtor and tells them what their house is worth. Gossipy neighbors spread the word about houses selling in the neighborhood. Many have their houses appraised to get home equity loans and can base their estimates on that. They can usually come pretty close.

Always ask the seller for a ballpark number or range. For example ask, "What would your house be worth in top condition? Just give me a ball-park." They'll say, "I'd guess about $100,000 to $120,000." Always use the lower number. In this case, I'd use $100,000 in my property analysis.

Some people might say, "Well it has a current value of $80,000." But the current value is meaningless. You're not going to sell it based on its current value. You're going to sell it wholesale to an investor/buyer who will fix it up and sell it. You need to know what it's going to sell for in mint condition.

On this first call, all you need is a ballpark number to make your first offer. As you will see later, your first offer will guarantee a profit, even if the seller or realtor is not entirely accurate. Before you ever close on any deal, you'll verify and certify both the value and the repair costs. I have closed deals every month for many years, and the ballpark numbers I got from my initial phone call with the seller or realtor have never steered me wrong.

Remember that you are not going to buy it on the first call. You just want to get your offer out to them in a way that leaves the door open for you to call them back or for them to call you back. Also, you want to get them into your database to be able to follow up with them. Remember, we want to "get them in the glue."

Ask the seller to ballpark the repair costs, too. On the repairs, you should use the *higher* number, if they give you a range. That way you are more conservative in your estimate.

Resist the temptation to lower the ballpark numbers you get from the seller because you want to be conservative. In the previous example, when a seller gives you a ballpark of $100,000 to $120,000, some people might want to be conservative and use $90,000 in the property analysis. Don't do it. Use $100,000. You're already being conservative by using $100,000. Lowering it by another $10,000 will result in your offer being $10,000 too low. Then your low-ball offer might be too low, which will make it more difficult to make a deal.

By the way, if you use the right verbiage when making your offers, the seller will not get offended. It's not what you say but also how you say it. If you would like to get a copy of the scripts I use when talking to sellers and realtors, you can get them by going to www.RealEstateDayTrading.com/Bonuses (see Figure 4.1).

How Much Will It Cost to Repair?

Sometimes, sellers will say, "I don't know" when you ask, "What's it going to cost to fix up the house"? Then you should come back with, "Just a ballpark." Sometimes no matter how hard they try, sellers can't come up with a number. If the seller still can't give you a range, then ask about the condition of the house: Does it need carpet? Has it been painted inside or outside lately? How's the roof? Does it need landscaping, windows, or a new front door? How does the kitchen look? Are the bathrooms in good shape?

I have found that most fixer-uppers typically need at least $10,000 in repairs, some need $15,000, and some need as much as $20,000 or more. From the answers to these questions you will get a pretty good idea of how much work needs to be done. Then you can pick one of these numbers to plug in to your instant property analysis. Don't worry about being exact at this point. You will verify everything later, so there's no risk.

Most realtors are reluctant to quote repair costs because they don't want to be held accountable. Just tell them you won't hold them to the number they give. I tell them, "Just give me a ballpark figure, and I won't hold you to it."

Most realtors have property disclosure reports from homeowners before they list the house. They know what shape the house is in and what repairs need to be made. They will tell you if you are persistent. However, if it is a bank-owned property, the bank is not required to fill out a property disclosure form for the realtor, as a general rule.

Name _____ Spouse _____

Property address _____ City _____ State _____

Zip _____ Phone (_____) _____-_____ Work # (_____) _____-_____

Spouse work # (_____) _____-_____ E-mail address _____@_____

Fax # _____

May we call you at work? *Yes No* **Best time to call:** AM ___ Afternoon ___ Evening __

How did you find out about us? _____

Type of home: Brick Wood frame DW SW Year built? _____ # of BR _____ # of BA

Style of home? _____ Tax value? _____ Sq. Ft. _____ Recent

improvements? _____

Repairs needed? _____ How much $? _____

Years owned? _____ Approx. value _____ How do you know? _____

How acquired? _____

1st mortgage bal._____ Rate _____ Paid to _____ Payment _____

How far behind? _____

2nd mortgage bal._____ Rate _____ Paid to _____ Payment _____

How far behind? _____

Are you in foreclosure? *Yes No* When is foreclosure date? _____ Other liens? _____

Name _____the house is in? _____ Anyone else making decisions? _____

Who?_____ Why are you selling? _____ What will you do if you don't sell? _____

How quickly do you want to sell? _____ What else should I be asking? _____

Are there any other problems with the house? _____

What will you do with the money? _____ Do you have any

other property to sell? _____

How long has it been for sale? _____ Had any offers? _____

How much? _____

Why didn't you take it? _____ Listed with realtor? _____ How much? _____

Vacant? _____ How long? _____ Rented? _____

Rent amount? _____ Tenants current? _____

Least amount you can take by Friday	1st x _____	Date _____
Least amount you can take by Friday	2nd x _____	Date _____
Least amount you can take by Friday	3rd x _____	Date _____
Least amount you can take by Friday	4th x _____	Date _____
Least amount you can take by Friday	5th x _____	Date _____

After the questions: Let me tell you a little about what we do. We buy____houses a month. We pay cash and can close in about one week. The advantage of selling your home to us (me or any other investor) is that we can close fast and we pay all cash. So, if you need to sell now and sell the property in an "as is" condition, we can help you. What is the least amount you can take for your house if we can close by Friday?_____. In order to pay cash and close in about a week, we need to be able to buy a house around 60% to 65% of the market value. This is because when we buy a house, we have to pay

FIGURE 4.1   For Sale by Owner Form/Script

the taxes, insurance, upkeep, rehab costs, interest, etc., and we have to advertise it, show it, and it usually takes 6 to 9 months to sell. We are looking for the buyer that you are looking for, only we are willing to wait 6 to 9 months. Based on what you told me about your house, we would probably need to be around_____.

Is that something that you think you could work with? It will always be no.
How close could you come?_____

Realtor Script for Calling on a Listing

Hi, my name is _____ and I was calling about the property at _____ address. Could you tell me who the listing agent is? _____ Great! May I speak with him/her? _____ (Not here) May I get their cell phone number? _____

(Listing agent on phone now)

Hi, my name is _____ and I am an investor. I saw your listing at _____ _____ address. Could you tell me a little about it?
(Ask the following questions in a conversational manner)
#BR _____ #BA _____ Sq. Ft. _____ Age _____ Is it vacant? _____ Is it bank owned? _____ How much work does it need? _____ _____ Dollar amount of work? (just a ballpark) _____ How much would it rent for? (just a ballpark) _____ How's the market there? _____ Would this be a good rental or is it better suited as retail property? _____ _____ What would it appraise for after repairs? (just a ballpark) _____ Could you sell it for that once I fix it up? _____ How long do you think it would it be on the market? _____ Have you had any offers on this house? _____ How long has it been on the market? _____ I know you work for the seller, but I also know that you want to get this house sold. What do you think it would take to buy this house with an all cash offer? _____ Do you work with many investors? As I mentioned, I'm an investor, and we buy about _____ houses a month and can pay cash and close fast. (If property is bank owned, have the realtor ask the bank asset manager if the bank owns any more properties in the area and mention that you may be interested in buying more than one for a discount.) Based on what you have told me, it looks like I need to be around _____ . Do you think we should make an offer on this house?_____
(You have been running your numbers while on the phone using the property analyzer and know what you can pay. Make an offer a little less than your max you can pay. If they say yes:) Let's make an offer on this house. Let's make an all cash offer of $ _____.
Make it subject to an inspection with a 15-day extension. Do you need to submit the offer in writing or do you want to just talk to the seller first? (If in writing:) The buyer is going to be _____ and/or assigns. (If they complain about the and/or assigns, tell them we never know what name we are going to title the property in until closing. You can also try to have

FIGURE 4.1   (Continued)

them make the offer in the name of _____ and/or financial partner) How much deposit do you need? _____ Just fax me the contract, and I will sign it and send you a check. Do you have anything else I need to be looking at? _____ Give them your contact information and always write your phone number and name in the corner of the offer. By the way, do you mind if I get your e-mail address so that we can stay in touch and I can buy some more property from you? _____

(They will always give it to you) Thanks a lot and I look forward to working with you. Have a great day.

Copyright © 2009 by Larry Goins. To customize this document, download Figure 4.1 to your hard drive from www.realestatedaytrading.com/bonuses. The document can then be opened, edited, and printed using Microsoft Word or another popular word processing application.

FIGURE 4.1   *(Continued)*

A THIRD QUESTION YOU NEED TO ASK

If you are working with an FSBO property, you also want to know the loan amount. You are looking for houses in need of repair that have a low loan balance or are owned outright, with no loan balance. Why? Because as a real estate day trader you are looking for houses you can buy at deep discounts from after-repair retail value of the house. For me, the *maximum allowable price* I will pay is 60 to 65 percent of the after-repair value. At this price, I can turnaround and resell the property to an investor for 70 percent of the after-repair price—and it will still be a good deal for them.

To buy houses at this kind of discount, the house must need repair work.

When analyzing a deal, always remember that the price you can offer is limited by the amount of the mortgage. If the mortgage amount is close to the after-repair value, you cannot buy the house at a good discount off the retail after-repair price. If the existing mortgage is higher than your maximum allowable price, then you can't make any money buying the house unless you do what is called a *short sale*. More on that in a minute. In this case you would have to buy at a price below the amount of the loan. But the lender wants to get paid and wouldn't agree to this deal. Figure 4.2 shows my Investment Property Analysis form.

SHORT SELLING IS NOT THE BEST WAY TO DAY TRADE HOUSES

If you're dealing with a preforeclosure, many times the mortgage on the property is too high to allow you to get the discounted buying price that you need to make a profit when you resell. In this case, you could try to get

Property Data

Address _____ City _____

State _____Zip _____

Bed/Bath _____ Sq. Ft. _____

Please circle all that apply: Brick   Vinyl   Wood   SFR   Duplex

Tax value: $ _____ Rented? Y N (Circle one) Rent (Projected rent, if vacant)

$ _____ /Month

Borrower Data

Borrower name _____ Co-borrower name _____

Company name _____ Phone _____ Fax _____

Borrower address _____ City _____ State _____ Zip _____

Borrower e-mail _____ @ _____Today's date ____ / ____ / _____

Please Disclose Your Intended Use of This Property: (Check one)

☐ Rehab and retail to owner/occupant
☐ Rehab and hold as a rental
☐ Wholesale to another investor
☐ Other (please specify) _____

Investment Data

After-repair value	$ _____
Purchase price	$ _____
Rehab cost	$ _____
Hard money closing cost	$ _____
Total cost	$ _____
Total investment to value	$ _____ % _____
LTV up to 70%	$ _____
Cash to close	$ _____

Initial Profit

After-repair value	$ _____
Total cost	$ _____
Total Equity/Profit	$ _____

FIGURE 4.2   Investment Property Analysis for Rehab Loan Submission Form

Cash flow/cashout

	75% $	80% $
LTV refinance loan amount	75% $	80% $
Minus closing costs ($1,750 + 1.5% of loan)	$	$
Minus hard money payoff	$	$
Equal tax-free cash out	$	$
Equity after refinance	$	$
Projected rent amount	$	$
Minus payment @ 30 years__%	$	$
Taxes (monthly estimate)	$	$
Insurance (monthly estimate)	$	$
Cash flow	$	$

After	Equity	Cash out	Cash flow
refinance	$_____ ____%	$_____	$_____/Mo/___/Year___

Notes _____

_____

_____

_____

_____

Notice and Disclosure: *Investors should verify estimated numbers independently. Financial Help Services, Inc.; Investors Rehab, Inc. its affiliates, officers, directors, and employees assume no liability either expressed or implied for such estimates or projections. This is not an offer for credit. All programs are subject to change, modifications, and deletions.*

Copyright © 2009 by Larry Goins. To customize this document, download Figure 4.2 to your hard drive from www.realestatedaytrading.com/bonuses. The document can then be opened, edited, and printed using Microsoft Word or another popular word processing application.

FIGURE 4.2   (*Continued*)

the lender to agree to a short sale—allowing the owner to sell to you at less than the mortgage, so the bank would write off a portion of the mortgage as a loss. You can attempt this, but it is a complex process that takes a long time. As a beginner, I wouldn't suggest attempting a short sale until you have a lot of experience and training in short selling. My good friend and trainer Dwan Bent-Twyford is the best I know at short sales. If you want to learn more about them, I suggest that you go to www.BrainPickaPro.com and listen to me interview her on short sales.

One of the keys to short selling is to find a house that is in extremely bad condition. Then you have some leverage with the lender. But remember, it won't happen overnight. It takes a while to complete a short sale. I believe in going after the low hanging fruit. There are many other houses out there that you can quickly buy at steep discounts and sell to your buyers/investors quickly. So why should you put a lot of time trying to climb up to the top of the tree to get a short sale for day trading when there are a lot of great deals just ripe for the picking on the lower branches? I have done short sales, and typically you can make more money on a short sale than you can on a day trading deal, but they take so long to complete that they don't work for day trading.

For day trading, the best strategy is to stick with houses that need repairs, that you can buy at a steep discount off the after-repair price, and resell to buyers/investors at 70 percent of after-repair value. That way you'll have buyers lined up to buy from you. If you step out of this business model and start acquiring houses that don't need repairs, or that are only slightly below market value, you could quickly get stuck with houses you can't sell. And that could be costly. Don't stray from the day trading model I've taught you.

Sometimes realtors will balk at giving you the loan balance. If they do, just say something like, "Jim, let me tell you how we work. We buy 8 to 10 houses every month. (If you are just getting started, you can leave out the number of houses you buy a month.) We pay all cash, and we can close in as soon as a week. I am prepared to give you an offer on your house right now, before I get off the phone with you. I need to know roughly how much the loan balance on this house is. Just a ballpark estimate will do." You can use the same speech when a seller or realtor hesitates to estimate the repairs or the after-repair value.

If the realtor refuses to give you an answer, ask him or her to contact the seller for permission. Realtors have a fiduciary responsibility to the seller if they are the listing agent. They may not give you the information unless the seller has advised them it is okay to tell a potential buyer. The realtor may be able to call the seller and ask if it is okay to tell you.

When you're talking to homeowners, in addition to the loan balance, you need to know how far behind they are on their payments. Instead of asking, "Are you behind on your payments?" ask "How far behind are you on your payments?" If they are not behind, they will tell you. If they are behind, they assume you already knew. This is a less embarrassing way of telling you that they are behind.

All of this is covered in the FSBO and realtor scripts (Figure 4.1). In Chapter 10, I will give you more detail about how to get the information you need and make them a good offer before you get off the phone. I'll also explain how to present a low offer in a way that will be respected and won't offend the realtor or seller or be rejected outright.

RUN THE NUMBERS

In my market, I have been able to wholesale houses for 70 percent of the appraised after-repair value. This may be the same or different in your market depending on market conditions, the price range of your houses, and what investors are willing to pay.

The 70 percent figure includes the purchase price, the cost of repairs, and closing costs. That means that I have to buy the property at a low enough price that when I add in all the repairs, the buyers closing costs, and my fee (more detail on this below), the total is less than or equal to 70 percent of market value.

When I can put together deals like that, investors/buyers will eat it up. It leaves a lot of room for them to make a big profit on the deal. That's why they line up for my deals. In order to cover these costs, and stay under 70 percent of the after-repair value, I have to be able to buy houses for about 60 to 65 percent of the after-repair value.

DO AN INSTANT PROPERTY ANALYSIS

Here's my eight-step instant property analysis system:

1. Let's assume the seller tells you the after-repair value is $100,000 to $120,000. Then we'll use $100,000 as our after-repair value.
2. We multiply $100,000 by 70 percent and that gives us an investment value of $70,000. This is the total amount of money that needs to be invested (my resale price plus the cost of repairs) to get the property in excellent condition, in order to sell it at retail prices or to rent or lease-option it to a tenant.
3. Next, I calculate the hard money closing costs. This is the expense your investor/buyer will incur to get a rehab loan from a hard money lender to repair the house. Sometimes an investor/buyer will not incur this cost. But I keep this in my instant property analysis to cover the worst-case scenario where the buyer has to get a hard money loan. Buyers who use their personal money to pay for repairs do even better because they won't incur this cost. In my experience, this cost is roughly 4 points or 4 percent of the $70,000 investment value. That works out to $2,800. Then I subtract this from the investment value. That brings me down to $67,200.
4. Then I estimate the cost of taxes, insurance, and attorney fees for houses in this price range and subtract it from the subtotal. These are the costs the buyer/investor will need to spend when he or she buys

the house from me. Based on my experience, these costs are $2,250 but it may be different in your area. I subtract $2,250 from $67,200, and I'm down to $64,950.

5. Now we need to subtract the repair costs. If the seller estimates repairs at $10,000 to $15,000, then I subtract $15,000. That leaves $49,950.

6. I also need to subtract the money I advanced for other expenses I will incur prior to buying the house. I always get an appraisal, which will cost about $400. I always get a title search. But most of the time the title company does not charge me for this. But if they do, it is about $100. With houses in extremely bad condition, I get a home inspection that costs me about $300. And if I am doing a physical close instead of an assignment, option, or simultaneous closing, I have to account for my closing costs. In this example, we need to account for the extra closing costs. That would be another $2,000.

   Let's assume all we need to include is the appraisal cost and the cost of the extra closing. That's $2,400. So I subtract $2,400 from $49,950, and the result is $47,550.

7. Now, I want to include my fee on the deal. I generally want to make 5 percent to 10 percent of the after-repair value. I start with 10 percent. This gives me some room to negotiate later if I need to lower the price. In this case, I'll start with 10 percent of $100,000 after-repair value. That's $10,000.

   So I subtract $10,000 from $47,550, and the result is $37,550. This is the maximum I can pay for this house and still make a profit for myself and offer my investor/buyer a deal on which he or she can make a profit. I cannot pay more than $37,550 for the house.

8. But my offer must be lower that that because I want to leave room for negotiation. So I offer about 12 to 15 percent below the maximum amount I can pay. I always use an odd number. An odd number makes it appear that I have calculated my costs carefully. In this case, I would offer $31,917 (see Figure 4.3) and negotiate from there.

If I had used a round number like $31,000 or $32,000, the seller would think I am just throwing out a number. I always want them to think I have done my homework and calculated the number down to the dollar.

Once you've gone through this a few times, it's easy. It's simple math. You can use Excel to set up a simple spreadsheet model to do all the calculations in seconds while you're still on the phone with the seller. Also, in my Ultimate Buying and Selling Machine course, I have an Ultimate Property Analyzer that does all of the work for you. The course is based on this book, and you can find out more at www.UltimateBuyingMachine.com.

After-repair value		$ 100,000
Investment value (70% of $ 100,000)		$ 70,000
Hard money closing costs (4% of $ 70,000)	($ 2,800)	$ 67,200
Taxes, insurance, attorney fees	($ 2,250)	$ 64,950
Repair costs	($ 15,000)	$ 49,950
Advance expenses and extra closing costs	($ 2,400)	$ 47,550
Day trader's fee (10% of $ 100,000)	($ 10,000)	
Maximum allowable price		$ 37,550
First offer ($ 37,550 − 15%)		$ 31,917

FIGURE 4.3   Sample Instant Property Analysis

This instant property analysis system works wonders and will help you double the number of offers you make and deals you close. Before we started using this system in 2004, we were able to make 7 offers a day. After we started using this system, we were able to make up to 17 offers a day.

BUY HOUSES SIGHT UNSEEN

Using this system, you can make offers on houses sight unseen, and eventually, you'll even be able to close on houses without ever seeing them. In the beginning, I recommend that you go look at houses before closing on them, especially if you are new to real estate and the property is located in your own city or area.

It won't be long before you will be able to complete the entire transaction without ever looking at the house. We do, and many of our students do it all the time, too. We now do all our business by phone, fax, FedEx, e-mail, and Internet. However, we do hire someone we trust to do this for us. Later, I'll show you how you can do this, too.

Once you have your day trading system set up, you can go into any market, in any city, anywhere in the country and buy and sell houses without seeing them. That is exactly what we do. We are buying and selling houses in new markets where we have never been every month.

AN EXCEPTION TO FIXER-UPPER PROPERTIES—INSTANT LANDLORD PROPERTIES

Whenever I buy a house in need of repair, the total amount invested after repairs, closing costs, and my fee must be no more than 70 percent of the after-repair value. However, occasionally I buy a house that's already in good shape and needs no repairs. That's another story.

If someone else has already bought it and fixed it up or it's in good condition, I can usually pay up to 80 percent sometimes 85 percent of the market value in a strong market or good rental market. I call these my instant landlord properties because you can flip them to an investor who can immediately rent them out for a positive cash flow. You want to leave plenty of room in case the investor needs to sell them quickly. At 80 percent to 85 percent, investors will always be able to sell the property if they need to.

If the property is in good condition and needs no repairs, the investor will not need a rehab loan and can probably get a traditional loan and then rent the property to someone for a positive cash flow. In this case when you do your instant property analysis, the closing costs will be the points needed to close a mortgage, not the points to secure a hard money rehab loan.

In today's market, it is hard for an investor to get 100 percent financing; it's also hard for them to get a cash-out refinance loan. Banks require a house to be *seasoned* before they will provide a refinance mortgage on it. Seasoning is how long you have owned the property before refinancing. Lenders have more stringent guidelines now and want an investor to own a property three to six months before getting a cash-out refinance loan.

I don't do many instant landlord deals simply because there aren't many out there that meet the criteria, and also, once your buyers get used to being able to buy a property from you having no more than 70 percent in it, they only want the 70 percent deals.

DAY TRADING LUXURY HOMES

Although you can make a lot more money per deal, I'm not a big fan of day trading luxury homes. When buying luxury homes, all the numbers change. You must buy luxury homes at a much larger discount simply because the values of a luxury home can change a lot depending on the appraisal. Appraisals of luxury homes are extremely inconsistent and unreliable. I usually deal in the low-income housing market where the appraisals do not vary too much from the norm—usually no more than 2 percent to 5 percent.

But appraisals of luxury homes can fluctuate by 20 percent or more up or down. You never know what you're going to get. If you use 70 percent of appraised value as a selling price target in luxury homes like I do in my lower-priced market, you would be taking too great a risk. You'd want to change that to allow for this wider margin of error in your instant property analysis.

If you find a luxury home that you can buy for 80 percent of appraised after-repair value, don't get too excited. It's not nearly enough of a discount. You've got to allow for an appraisal that will wipe out some of the discount margin. You need a better deal than that, at least a price that's 60 percent, or maybe 50 percent, of market value. The most you will be able to wholesale the property for is 70 percent to 75 percent of market value. As a general rule, I do not buy a luxury home unless I can get it at 50 percent to 60 percent of after-repair value including all of the costs involved. I learned this from luxury home expert and author Frank McKinney. You can learn more about Frank and luxury home investing by listening to me interview him at www.BrainPickaPro.com.

THREE TYPES OF DEALS

To summarize, when you're buying houses from distressed sellers, you are likely to encounter three types of deals:

1. *Houses with little equity that need no repairs:* Homeowners in default are looking to sell their house fast just to get out of their loan. In the case of a house in good condition, if the loan balance is close to the market value of the house, there is nothing you can do for them unless you can negotiate a short sale, which can take time.
2. *Houses with more than 20 percent equity that are in good repair:* You can usually pay up to 80 percent to 85 percent of the market value and flip these to a buyer/investor who can immediately rent them out for a positive cash flow. These are the instant landlord houses that I described previously. If the 20 percent equity house is in need of repair, you should pass on it. The cost of repairing the house will eliminate the possibility of making a profit.
3. *Houses with more than 50 percent equity:* These are the best kinds of houses for day traders. With houses like this, there is a good chance that the total amount invested after repairs, closing costs, and your fee will be no more than 70 percent of the after-repair value.

That's why you need to know the loan amount. Your bread-and-butter houses should have a low loan balance or are owned outright with no loan balance. These are the kinds of houses you can buy at a steep discount and sell quickly to a buyer/investor. Most are in bad condition, and some are vacant.

Sometimes you'll be fortunate enough to find houses like this that are in good condition because of preforeclosure, divorce, people who are paying two mortgages, heirs, involuntary owners, absentee owners, and so on. If you're able to negotiate such a steep discount, you'll find that the house needs some major repair work in most cases.

DAY TRADING NOT INVESTING

Keep in mind that you are not investing your money in real estate when you are a day trader. Sure you will sometimes write a check temporarily to close the deal. But you will have already lined up a buyer and will get your money back immediately after they close, often the very same day.

MAKE YOUR DEALS IRRESISTIBLE TO BUYERS

I've shown you how to evaluate houses instantly and make strong offers that will ensure that you make deals in which you and your investor/buyer will make money. Here's how you can make your deals absolutely irresistible. My students and I are the only ones I know of doing this. This will make your buyers choose your houses over your competitor's and incite them to make offers on your houses sight unseen in two hours or less.

This is important because in real estate day trading, time is critical. Once you get a contract to buy a house, you must find a buyer to resell it to within 30 days. So once you sign a contract, the clock is ticking. If you can't sell in 30 days, the deal is dead and you lose your deposit. It's not the end of the world. But you don't want this to happen too often. You'll lose good deals, you'll lose valuable opportunities that could make you a $5,000 paycheck, and you'll lose your $500 deposit.

In day trading, your only risk is your $500 earnest money deposit that you provide when you make an offer. I'll teach you some ingenious techniques to protect yourself from ever losing your $500 deposit. We add some important clauses to our contracts that protect us for any risk of loss in making offers on houses sight unseen.

With most real estate wholesalers who aren't day trading, once the offer is accepted and the contract signed, they immediately try to sell the house *as is*. When you buy or sell a house as is, it means there are no warranties, and the buyer is stuck with it no matter how many problems it has. Most wholesalers push buyers to hurry up and make up their minds because of the 30-day time limit the seller has given them.

Therefore most investors view deals from wholesalers with a healthy skepticism. They are cautious and usually take the time to inspect the property thoroughly before making an offer on an as-is house. If they buy it, they are stuck with it, no matter how bad or unprofitable it is.

We do something different. We make our houses easier for the investor/buyer to evaluate and less risky. They are motivated to sign contracts on our houses sight unseen in less than a few hours. When an investor buys from a typical wholesaler who hasn't done his or her homework, and the investor finds out after the fact that the house wasn't as good a deal as he thought, he will never buy another property from that wholesaler again. That does not happen with us because we make sure our buyers/investors get a good deal.

First, we make sure our contract to buy the house contains three clauses that protect us and allow us to back out of the deal if we need to. (These are described in Chapter 9). Then we do something that no other wholesalers do.

Once we sign a contract with the seller, we immediately send a rehab contractor to thoroughly inspect the house and give us an accurate estimate of what needs to be done and exactly how much it's going to cost. Remember, we have no intention of repairing this house. Even though we will not repair the property, the buyer will, and many times the buyer will use the contractor we had write up the inspection repair list. That is why contractors are willing to give us a free estimate on the needed repairs.

An accurate estimate of repairs is of great value to our investor/buyer. The inspection uncovers any hidden problems that are not visible during a casual observation. The estimate tells us what needs to be done to make it attractive enough to easily sell it at full market price.

Then we give an appraiser the rehab contractor's report and ask the appraiser to give an accurate appraisal of the after-repaired value. We do all this before we offer the house to our investors/buyers. Time is critical, so we work with contractors and appraisers who can work fast. We can usually get this done within a week. Then we announce the property to our investors/buyers.

Now our investors/buyers have all the information they need to make an informed decision without seeing the house. A licensed rehab contractor has inspected the house. A licensed appraiser has given an accurate appraisal. These are professionals who know their business and work with houses every day. They know their stuff. Our investors/buyers don't need to drive to the house and make a guess about the repairs and the value. We have had professionals do this for them. We have included this information to reduce the risk to our buyers and make it easier to buy. Our investors/buyers can immediately make a decision to buy our houses sight unseen.

You will find that many of the buyers you will get on your buyer's list will not even live in the city or state where they are buying property from you. They are buying properties site unseen outside of their area, and we want to make it easy for them to buy.

If you would like to see what one of our listings looks like you can visit www.InvestorsRehab.com and look at any of our properties to see the inspection report and appraisal. You can also sign up to get on our buyers list to get automatic e-mail notification of our properties as they become available. In the following chapter, I'll show you how you can find motivated buyers who will jump at offers like this.

CHAPTER 5

USE THE INTERNET AND WEB 2.0 TO BUILD A DATABASE OF MOTIVATED BUYERS

I have told you the kind of houses your investors/buyers are looking for, how to make offers on these houses, and how to make your deals irresistible. Now I'm going to explain how you can build a database of motivated buyers who will buy your houses even before you close on them. You want to have a buyer lined up to buy your house the same day you buy it from the seller. You will buy and sell in the same day. That's day trading. That's how we are able to make 5 to 10 $5,000 plus paydays every month.

Trying to sell houses without having buyers lined up is like my pastor Kenny Ashley says, "That's like having two ticks and no dog." You don't want to have houses for sale and no buyers lined up.

WHY YOU NEED A DATABASE OF BUYERS BEFORE YOU EVER TALK TO SELLERS OR REALTORS

In setting up your real estate day trading business, the first thing you want to do is to create a database of motivated investors/buyers who are very interested in buying the houses you are selling. This is important because in real estate day trading, time is critical. When you make offers and get contracts to buy houses, as I'll explain in more detail later, you will typically have 15 days to inspect the property, get an appraisal, and find a buyer;

45

and 30 days total to close. The rehab contractor does the inspection and estimates the cost of making repairs. The appraiser gives you a certified appraisal of the after-repair value. *You* find the buyer. It's all got to be done in 15 days, which is typically the inspection period of your contract.

I strongly advise you to find buyers before you start buying houses. If you wait until you have a house under contract to start looking for a buyer, it will be difficult to do in such a short time. It will take days to run ads, sort through all the replies, and get offers. It's too stressful.

The other factor is confidence. It's going to be difficult to make strong offers with conviction if you don't have buyers lined up and a source of funding for the deal. In my day trading system, you must have both funding and buyers ready before you start talking to sellers and realtors. Realtors are going to ask you if you have the funds to close. If you are not certain, they will notice. And if you tell a realtor you've got to find a buyer first before closing, they'll drop you fast. From a confidence point of view, it's best to have funding lined up. But there are many ways to start without any cash or credit, as I will show you later.

To be successful in real estate day trading, you need to have a group of investors/buyers ready, willing, and able to buy your houses at a moment's notice. That's why you need a database of buyers before you start looking for houses to buy. Then, when you make a good deal with a seller or realtor to buy a house, you know you have hundreds of motivated buyers who are eager to take it off your hands.

Once you have a database, you can contact them whenever you have a house for sale and know that they will be ready to buy quickly. The good news is motivated buyers are easy to find because there are so many of them and they are hungry for deals. Wouldn't it be great to have a database of them?

WHAT IS A DATABASE?

First, I want to explain what a database is and what it can do.

In its simplest form, a database is a list. It could be a list of customers, prospects, former customers, friends, or relatives. A Christmas card list is a database. Your personal information is stored in many databases. The property tax rolls for your county are in a database and so are voter's registration, social security, and motor vehicle registration records.

Information contained in any database usually includes names, addresses, telephone numbers, fax numbers, cell phone numbers, e-mail addresses, web sites if any. You could even keep track of the history of transactions with each individual, although we do not. There are many software programs designed specifically for building, maintaining, and using databases.

In your database, you should record all the important information about your buyers such as: name, address, title, company name, telephone number, fax number, cell number, e-mail address, and web site address. You will probably also want to list other information, such as the types and locations of houses that interest them and previous conversations you have had with them. Then when you contact them, you can refer to your previous conversations and interactions.

Types of Database Software You Can Use

There are dozens of customer relationship management programs, both online and PC based that you can use to build a customer contact database. ACT! 2008 Contact Manager is one of the most popular. Prophet and Chaos are some other good ones.

I actually started out with ACT! Contact Manager many years ago and used it for several years. It really helped me to streamline my business. I kept details about all my buyers at my fingertips so I could access the files on any of my contacts, including important buyers, realtors, and suppliers. I set up a call reminder system to notify me of important calls, meetings, and to dos, so that nothing slips through the cracks. It is crucial to be able to immediately see tasks, meetings, and priorities, in a single view and drill down for details.

Automate or Die

After a few years, I switched to an online contact manager—1 Shopping Cart. I wanted to automate my contact system. And 1 Shopping Cart is more automated than having your own computer program, like ACT!

For example, if you have your own program and someone wants to unsubscribe from your e-mail list, you have to go in manually and unsubscribe that person. However, if you use an online service, when someone clicks on the link in your e-mail to unsubscribe, it happens automatically. You simply receive an e-mail notifying you that the person is unsubscribed. Another advantage of an online system is that you can access it from anywhere on any computer.

I didn't want to continue to contact buyers manually. I wanted to be able to preprogram my system to contact my buyers and build my company's image without me being involved. Autoresponders were the answer. And 1Shopping Cart has an autoresponder built in. A Weber is another popular online contact management system with autoresponder capability.

An online database service allows you to access it from any computer that has Internet capabilities. I use my own web site that I created just for day trading my properties, which has all these tools built in. To see what it looks like you can visit my day trading site at www.InvestorsRehab .com. If you would like to see a demo site like mine, you can visit www .UltimateInternetMarketingMachine.com.

The key to increasing your productivity and your cash flow is automation.

I use other people, Web 2.0 technology, outsourcing, employees, virtual assistants, and joint ventures. And because of that, I day trade 5 to 10 or more houses every month without tying up my personal time. Now I am free to take on new challenges, spend more time with my family, and basically enjoy life to the fullest. To live the life of a real estate day trader, you have to do whatever you have to do to get the work done—without you doing it.

USE AUTORESPONDERS TO STAY IN CONSTANT CONTACT

An autoresponder is software that automatically responds to e-mail that is sent to you or sent out when someone goes into your database. It can be set up as a single e-mail response or multiple responses delivered at various intervals. The neat thing is, once you set it up, it's all automatic. You can set up a response to an inquiry from your web site or set up a response from someone who sends you an e-mail while you are out of town.

Everyone has received e-mail from an autoresponder. Have you ever signed up for a teleconference, webinar, or a free report on the Internet and received an automatic instant e-mail? These are all examples of e-mails sent by autoresponders. An autoresponder helps you become a seller who never sleeps and is the cheapest personal assistant you will ever hire.

Your autoresponder, combined with savvy marketing, is the speediest way to immediately boost business! It's an immense time saver that turns web site visitors into buyers. It gives you a huge advantage. Not many real estate investors are following up with every realtor, investor/buyer, and seller/owner every week. It can be the difference between having a real estate business that works hard for you and you constantly having to work hard for your real estate business. That's why autoresponders are so vital.

You can focus your autoresponder messages on the exact needs of your buyers, your realtors, your owners/sellers, and your suppliers. You can send a preset series of e-mail messages and have them automatically delivered monthly, weekly, daily, or even more often. In fact in my course called the *Ultimate Buying and Selling Machine!* that this book is based on, I have already written 12 months of autoresponders to follow up with your contacts. You can find out more and listen to a free teleconference and get a 10-part ebook by going to www.UltimateBuyingMachine.com. Then you are free to spend your time doing more productive things like making offers, closing deals, and depositing $5,000 plus paychecks in your bank account.

The Fortune Is in the Follow-Up

Use your online contact management system that includes autoresponder software to e-mail, call, or direct mail your buyers or other contacts at any time. If you have an exciting new house for sale at a very appealing and profitable price, you can send an e-mail blast out to your buyer list. If you're up against a deadline and you've got to sell fast, you can send out an e-mail and get two or three offers in less than an hour. If you need an appraisal in Bend, Oregon, in one day, you can blast your message out to your supplier list and line up eager appraisers who want to get the job done for you. There's no limit to the uses.

Using an online contact management system like 1Shopping Cart or A Weber, you can get a web site and domain name for your real estate day trading business. Then you can create an opt-in box to collect names and e-mail addresses from your web site. In addition to autoresponders, contact management systems have database management, e-mail broadcast, web forms to put on your web site, a shopping cart, and much more. If you use a shopping cart, you can literally set it up so that your buyers can pay their deposits by credit card. Is that great or what?

Branding with Name, Logo, and Business Cards

First, you should create a name, get a logo, and decide on a company color or colors. This way you can brand your name and company in all of your marketing. Don't shortchange yourself; do it right. Image is very important whenever you are marketing to the public. They don't know you. The only way they can know you is from what you show them. Use a name and logo that will impress on them that you are someone who is a professional. You can get a very nice logo designed for under $80. One popular logo design service is www.logostogo.com.

Also, order some business cards. Business cards are one of the best and lowest-cost forms of marketing that I do. And you can't possibly do any networking without a business card. If you are in business, then you need a business card. I want you to be unique. I used to have one that was printed on both sides and had a picture of me on it. It doesn't matter who you are; a picture on your business card will make people hang on to your card longer. I recently saw the back of a card where an investor had copied part of a $20 bill; when it was lying facedown it looked like a folded $20 bill. This would be pretty easy to do.

Be different when designing your business cards: Some people have magnetic business cards, some use fluorescent colors. I have heard that fluorescent yellow cards are working very well for people. The point is that you need to hand them out to everybody. They are especially useful in attracting and locating motivated sellers, which I'll cover in the next chapter. I use million-dollar-bill business cards in my networking, marketing, and prospecting. You can get these at www.MillionDollarSource.com or www.Madow.com.

I consider myself a good marketer, and I am always looking for better ideas. Recently, I was driving to Macon, Georgia, to speak at the Investors Association when my car ran out of gas. So there I was on the side of the interstate with a bright red H2 Hummer going nowhere fast. I tried to call my office to see if they could call a service station to bring some gas to me, but I didn't know where I was exactly. There were no exits in sight and no mile markers around. I just stood there for a few minutes watching cars pass me by at 70 mph.

I thought to myself, "How can I use my marketing skills to get someone's attention?" After sitting there for about 15 minutes trying to figure it out, it hit me. I got out of the vehicle, pulled out a $20 bill, walked back to the side where the gas tank was, took off the gas cap, and stood there waving my $20 bill and pointing at the gas cap. Within two minutes, someone stopped, took me to the next exit to get a gas can full of gas, brought me back, and even helped me get the car started. I made it on time to speak that night.

The moral of the story is you should always be thinking about how to get the attention of your prospects. I had to market to the drivers on the interstate. I was successful because I gave them something that they wanted.

In this case, I showed them the *money*. That motivated them big time. By the way, I actually gave the guy who stopped $100 for helping me out!

WAYS TO BUILD YOUR BUYERS DATABASE

There are three main ways to build a database of motivated buyers: marketing, networking, and prospecting. You can do all three methods online or offline.

Marketing

Marketing is anything that makes the phone ring or someone contact you. This includes running ads, displaying or distributing flyers and signs, mailing postcards, and more. These are your best kinds of leads. Prospects are coming to you, rather than you going to them. This puts you in a position of power, and it is much easier than cold-calling somebody. In other words, when the phone rings, and you answer the phone, "Hi, how can I help you?" This means that *you* are helping *them*. They are trying to sell you; you are not trying to sell them.

However, if you are calling about their sign, their house that's for sale, or calling them because they had a foreclosure notice that you found out about, then you are trying to sell them on selling you their house. They are in the position of power.

Newspaper Classified Ads   If you want to get every investor in town to contact you, just run an ad in the "Investment Properties For Sale" section of your newspaper. A while back, we ran an ad for a three-bedroom, two-bath house in Memphis, Tennessee, that had extensive fire damage. Because most buyers were afraid of it, we were able to pick it up for just $27,000. The repairs were estimated to be $20,000, and we listed it for $32,000, with an after-repair value of $88,000. This was a great deal where a buyer could easily make $34,000 after the repairs.

We placed an ad in the Investment Properties section that said: "Handyman Special, Cheap, Cash." We got lots of phone calls. You can do the same thing.

But what if you are just starting out and don't have a house to sell? What can you do to get buyers lined up ahead of time?

There are two things you can do. You can sell another investor's property just to build your list and to practice talking to buyers. It is good experience and can give you confidence. You have nothing to lose, and the person whose house you are selling has nothing to lose. And you get to add all these investors/buyers to your database for later when you have a real deal for them. You may even be able to get paid a fee for doing this if your state laws allow it.

Even if you don't have a house for sale you can still run the "Handyman Special, Cheap, Cash" ad. Have an answering service or call capture service handle all the calls. Give the operators a script to prescreen your callers, get their contact information, and tell them you will phone or e-mail them the next time you have a great deal.

Free Online Classified Ads   The Internet is loaded with free online classified sites where you can post your real estate classified ad for free. We now use the Internet for all our classified ads for building our buyers database. I suggest that you use your e-mail address instead of your phone number so that you can simply add them to your e-mail contact list and never have to talk to them. And if you have your own web site, you could just put it in the ad to send people to the site to sign themselves up automatically. This is the way we do things now. However, if you want to prescreen prospects, list only your phone number and have your answering service or call capture service screen them, put the information in a database, and e-mail it to you. Then you can pick the best buyers to contact immediately.

The most well-known classified service is Craigslist.com. You can run your "Handyman Special, Cheap, Cash" ad under the "Real Estate For Sale" section. People who read your ad will be able to click through to another page where you can give all the details.

Craigslist is not the only free classified ad site. There are dozens of them. Here are several that I use: InetGiant.com, FreeAdLists.com, USFreeAds .com, vast.com, oodle.com, postlets.com, and DomesticSale.com.

It would take hours of your time to post to all the sites out there. To use your time more effectively, you can outsource this work to a professional online posting company that will post your house listings to all sites for you and direct the leads back to you for building your list and selling your houses. One professional online posting company is PostingForYou.com. You can Google "free classified ads" to find more places to post and also Google "ad posting service" to find services like postingforyou.com to place your ads.

Do this, and you will build a powerful and valuable investor database in no time. I know investors who have built their database to literally thousands of investors using this one idea.

Real Estate Advertising on eBay   Run a classified ad in eBay to find motivated investors to add to your database. Just go to realestate.ebay.com to post a property or just run an ad. You can get loads of national exposure for your "Handyman Special, Cheap, Cash" ad. The current (at the time of printing) ad price for an ad to run 30 days is $150 and 90 days is $300.

Marketing Web Site   Build your database of buyers using your own web site. This is a great way to build an amazing database of investors effortlessly. First you need to register your domain name. Then you build or buy a web site. Then you write a valuable informative report to give away free for people who sign in to your web site. After that, you build traffic to your site so that investors come to your site and sign in to your database to receive your free report. You can build traffic by running free online classified, banner ads on high-traffic real estate sites, and pay-per-click ads on Google Adwords and Yahoo Search Marketing.

If you don't already have a registered domain name, register "your name" dot-com like BobSmith.com. If you have a business name be sure to register that as well. You can go to a web site like www.godaddy.com to register the name. It doesn't cost much money at all (approximately $8, $9, or $10 per year). We always register ours for 10 years. That way we know it is going to be around for a while.

Once you have a domain name, then you need a web site. You do not have to be technologically advanced to build and edit your web site. There are many online services where you can get some cheap web sites. And some are even free. They might not have all the features you need to effectively run your business, but they may be a place to start until you close lots of deals and make money. You can have your own web site in minutes. My company offers a web site based on my day trading system. You can get all the details at www.UltimateInternetMarketingMachine.com.

Now you need the software to handle the traffic, process requests for your eBook, add contact information to your database, and process deletions from your database automatically. There are many services that do this. AWeber.com is a popular one. And 1Shopping Cart also offers a professional online marketing system that includes everything you need—shopping cart, autoresponders, eBook delivery, diagnostics to track your ads, and more.

Now you need to create a free report that investors want. I have written free reports to find investors/buyers: The 12 Deadly Mistakes Investors Make and How to Avoid Them; Secrets of Selling Your House in 7 Days; Lenders, How to Earn 7%–10% Secured by Real Estate; How to Buy a

Home with No Money Down. If you would like to use one of my free reports, you can download it for *free* by going to www.realestatedaytrading .com/bonuses and clicking on Free Reports.

Free reports are a great tool that you can use to entice your visitors to hand over their contact information. You are offering valuable information they want. When they request the free report, they are automatically added to your database.

Once you have a report, convert it into a PDF document, and upload it to your web marketing site to be automatically delivered to everyone who signs in to your site and requests the report. Their contact information will be automatically recorded in your database. They'll receive your follow-up autoresponder e-mail messages and announcements of houses you have for sale.

Follow-up is very important. Once you capture a lead, you *have* to follow up with them. By using the built-in autoresponders, this will happen automatically. Contacts will receive preloaded messages as frequently as you want. Then when you have a great house to offer, send them a special announcement describing the deal. They will respond in record numbers.

You can go the next step as I have done and completely automate the whole process by listing the properties for sale on your web site complete with pictures, descriptions, and all the related documents they need to make a decision. You can post as many photos and documents as needed to sell your property. You can create a detailed listing on your properties that answers all your buyer's questions so they can submit a contract on the property without contacting you. Just think of the time it's going to *save you*!

When they are ready to make you an offer, direct them to a web page with complete instructions on making an offer. This tells your visitors exactly how they can buy your property right there in the comfort of their own home! It includes everything the potential buyer needs to know about your property in order to make an informed decision and includes a downloadable contract for them to fax to you. They can wire or PayPal you the deposit. You can make the entire deal over the Internet using your web site. This is the future of real estate using Web 2.0 technology.

You can also use the autoresponders to build a strong support team. Autoresponders are a key component to building your dream team of realtors, appraisers, contractors, and lenders.

This is a powerful tool for building your database of potential buyers who want to receive instant e-mail alerts when you list a new property on your site. When these subscribers get your new listing alert . . . they will be competing for your property at the same time! You will often have many buyers for the same property at the same time. Then all you have to do is pick one and tell the others you've put them on the backup list in case the first buyer falls through or decides to drop out. What a great position to be in.

Remember, you don't need a web site marketing system to day trade houses. You can easily do this business without a web site. But if you want to go to the next level and be able to day trade houses in two hours or less automatically, then you will need to have a web site. Start getting into the game by making offers, getting contracts, closing deals, and getting big checks. Once you see how the business works, then take the next step and power up your marketing with a marketing web site.

Networking

Networking involves personal contact with people you meet through membership groups and social interactions.

Investors Clubs   The most productive form of networking, one that costs the least amount of money but produces the best results is joining your local real estate investing club or association, if you have one. When you start out in real estate day trading, the fastest way to become successful is to become a big fish in a small pond. The fastest way to do this is to join and participate in your local real estate club. Start out as a volunteer. Do whatever you can to help. Become an officer of the club, attend all the meetings, and get known around town. People will begin to recognize you and trust you. And you'll learn a lot about who does what and who to go to for legal assistance, appraisals, and financing. You'll learn who the investors are and what kinds of houses they are buying. When you go to these events, be sure to hand out your business card and collect the business cards of the buyers.

Just about every city has a REIA Club, a Real Estate Investors Association, or a Landlord Association. Join them all. I cannot tell you how valuable this resource is. If you don't have a club in your area, I would suggest going to the next nearest town that does to learn what they are all about. Or, if you don't have one in your town, then start one. You can find a local group or get information on starting one by contacting www.nationalreia.com. They will help you start a club in your area. Your local club is a great source of networking for buyers, sellers, rehabbers, appraisers, attorneys, realtors, hard money lenders, private investors, property managers, insurance agents, and mortgage brokers.

Anyone working in real estate needs to be involved in their local real estate group. It is well worth your time to network and learn from other people. You learn who the players are, who is buying property and who is not, who the talkers are, who the doers are, who to do business with, and who to stay away from. Once you get involved in the leadership of the club, all the new investors will be contacting you about helping them with their deals.

This is how I became a trainer and eventually created the Day Trading system. I was asked by the founder of my local association Allon Thompson of Metrolina REIA to get involved in the group. I joined, became a volunteer, and was eventually elected president for two years. I became what I call a "big fish in a small pond." I was known as a player in the business who was doing deals. I was one of the local go-to guys to bring deals to, and it all started because I volunteered at my local association. Thanks Allon!

Yahoo and Google E-Mail Marketing Groups   There are real estate investor groups all over the country. Some are large, and some are small; some are moderated and some are unmoderated. It is easy to join these groups. Simply go to www.yahoo.com or www.google.com and look for the section on groups. Then search for groups about real estate investing and sign up. There are currently over 1,600 groups with an interest in real estate investing that have anywhere from a few members to several thousand members in each group.

You can also just type "groups.yahoo.com" or "groups.google.com" in your browser to go to pages for the groups. Subscribe to as many groups as you can; it's all free. You can be in touch with investors/buyers in every part of the country with the click of a mouse.

The unmoderated ones are the easiest to deal with. You can send e-mails to the entire group describing houses you have for sale, giving details, and asking for interested investors to contact you. You can sell your properties to them without ever meeting them. Even if they don't buy immediately, they might buy in the future. Be sure to save every one of these e-mail addresses and other contact information in your database. Then your autoresponder messages will keep in touch with them for you.

Moderated groups are a little trickier. Your e-mail will be tracked by the moderator for several weeks after joining to make sure you are not spamming the list, with irrelevant offers that have nothing to do with real estate. So be very careful and make every posting relevant to the conversations being discussed within the group. Then after several weeks, perhaps at the end of a posting to the group, you could mention a house that you have for sale, as an afterthought, but not the main theme of the message. Some groups and forums consider commercial posts to be spam and delete them, which could get you expelled from the group. You can usually publish your web site and a brief description of what you do in your signature at the end of your postings without that being considered spam.

Yahoo and Google are not the only web portals with groups. Some other sites that host real estate groups are AOL, GroupSense, About.com, MSN.com, and eBay.com.

Social Networking Sites   There are three main types of social networking web sites: personal, professional, and real estate-focused.

Personal networking sites (such as MySpace, FaceBook, Tribe, and Friendster.com) enable people to socialize, find business contacts, talk sports, or meet other people.

MySpace has literally millions of members, and it is free. It is not a dating site but a networking site for people of all ages and backgrounds. Every major investor, trainer, realtor, and even celebrities and politicians have a MySpace page. You can sign up, create your own web page on MySpace, and then invite friends to come to your page and sign up as your friend. You can even list certain keywords like (real estate investing, foreclosures, etc.) and then search for other members who have those keywords in their pages. This is a great way to build your buyers list, promote your properties, and network with other like-minded people and it is all *free*!

There are also professional sites that take a business-only approach and don't allow people to connect directly with others if they don't already know them. The most common professional/business sites include Ziggs, ZoomInfo, LiveJournal, ZeroDegrees, LinkedIn, Plaxo Pulse, and Ryze Business Networking.

When you become a member of LinkedIn, for example, you can create a profile of yourself. You can use that profile to describe yourself, your occupation, industry, and professional background. You can use this professional profile to describe yourself as a real estate investor who wants to link up with other real estate investors. Once you're a member, you can perform keyword searches to return matches based on your interest in real estate investing. Then you can invite all the other real estate investors in the entire network to link to you and become a part of your inner circle. Once someone agrees to be part of your network, they are permitted to communicate freely with the members of your group by exchanging leads, ideas, and advice, and doing business with each other. You can send bulletins out to your circle of real estate investors describing a house you have for sale. It's your own private real estate insiders group.

You can also search for people within the LinkedIn community by name. However, in order to contact a particular person, you would have to first invite that person to link with you. It's a great way to build a solid network of buyers, lenders, joint venture partners, and support professionals who can work for you and send you leads about investors and sellers.

The more connections a person has, the bigger his or her network becomes. But the possibilities are endless because you have the potential to reach many more people besides the ones you are connected with. That's because the people you are connected to have networks of their own that spread out into a gigantic web of interlinked connections. For example, you might be personally connected to 377 people, but through the network of those people, you could potentially reach 356,000 people. The average member's network contains an estimated 60,000 professionals.

Most LinkedIn members join the network as a result of receiving an invitation from someone else who has already joined. However, if you want to join without invitation, you can go to the web site, create a profile, and use a feature that compares the e-mails in your e-mail address book to e-mail addresses in the network. It finds people you already know who are LinkedIn members for you to connect to.

The last type is real estate-focused networking sites. There are numerous sites that can connect people who are involved in real estate, enabling them to meet online to talk shop, get advice, and buy and sell properties. Join as many of these as you can, and start using them to build your database of investors. Here are the names of a few of them: ConnectionTree.com, Money4Investors.com, TheCreativeInvestor.com, and RealEstateInvestor .com.

Real Estate Auctions   You will also want to attend auctions to be able to build your buyers list. Many people at real estate auctions are investors. Take your business card and be prepared to hand it out to everyone there. And get other investors' cards and tell them that you also have properties available to investors. You can find many of these auction sites online. Just search "real estate auctions" with your city name or visit www.auctioneers.org.

Prospecting

Prospecting is anything that requires you to research the names of prospective investors and make the first phone call or e-mail contact. When contacting investors, the purpose of your call is to sell them a house or add them to your database of possible buyers.

Explain that you are an investor who specializes in single-family houses that are in need of repair in low- to middle-income areas. Tell them that you can supply them with houses at a price that will give them a 30 percent discount from the appraised after-repair value, after the repairs and closing costs are paid. Tell them that you have great deals that they can make lots of money on. Tell them that the houses that you advertise are all preinspected and preappraised. Ask if you can put them on your database to send them notifications of houses you have for sale.

At first, you can make all the calls to investors yourself. Later, just develop a script and hire someone to call them for you. Later in this book, I'll show you how you can automate this whole process. Who should you call? Here are some suggestions.

"I Buy Houses" Signs   Drive around your town and look for "I Buy Houses" signs. Write down the numbers and call them later.

Online Classifieds, Newspaper Ads, and Realtor Sites   Scan many online sources for investors selling houses. You don't have to touch a newspaper in order to scan the classifieds. You can do it all online. There are a number of online services that help you scan the classifieds. My favorite is newsdirectory.com. From this site you can find just about any newspaper that is available online. You can search the classifieds in many newspapers using keywords, by size, location, or price range of the houses you want. Use a wide search of houses in your area. Then scan for the ones being offered for sale by investors.

Sometimes it's hard to tell if an ad is from a realtor or an investor. Look for ads selling houses on a lease option or rent-to-own basis. These are usually investors. Also look for ads that offer down payment and closing cost assistance. Often newly remodeled homes are for sale by investors. These investors will soon be looking for other low-priced houses in need of repair to fix up and sell. And you can supply them.

Look for single-family homes for sale. Another category to look at is houses for rent. Owners who are renting houses are usually investors and are good prospects to buy more houses to fix up and rent out.

Check out eBay real estate classifieds to find investors selling houses on eBay. They need to buy houses in order to sell them on eBay. You can put them in your database and let them know when you have a profitable deal for them. Go to eBay and click the links to real estate, then click residential.

After that search by state. All the listings in your state will display. Most of these are posted by investors. You can look at all the properties they have for sale to see the feedback from others who have done business with them. You can even sign in and contact the seller.

Also scan Craigslist and the other free real estate classified web sites and realtor sites like realtor.com.

Search Google   Go to Google and search the words "sell my house" and add your city to the search first (e.g., "Charlotte Sell My House"). Look at the different ads for the local realtors and also for the investors selling property. These investors are good prospects to buy a house from you. Call or e-mail them about adding them to your database for announcements about investor houses you have for sale. You can also search other keywords and include your city name: Charlotte foreclosure, Charlotte buy my house, Charlotte sell house fast, and so on. Contact all the investors that turn up in these searches. They are your potential buyers.

TABBED BROWSING TO SPEED UP YOUR SEARCHING

Tabbed browsing basically means that you do not have to open up a whole separate window for every web site that you go to. You are able to open a group of tabs so they all load at the same time. This saves a tremendous amount of time. Let's say you want to look at all the newspapers in your area every day to find investors to add to your database and buy your houses. Instead of having to do a new search every day, you can use tabbed browsing to create an online catalog of tabbed pages to add to your bookmarks.

From then on, all you have to do is go to your bookmarks and open the folder that contains the tabbed web sites. Then look at each tab to find what you are looking for. You can do this when searching for investors/buyers to sell houses to and when searching for sellers and realtors to buy houses from. You can also set up tabs that have web sites of contractors, appraisers, and other support members to add to your dream team.

I search about 11 different newspapers in our area. First, I go to newsdirectory.com and use that site to locate all the newspapers in my area. Then I created a group called "My Newspapers" that opens to the real estate section of the classifieds in every newspaper in my market. I don't have to start over and sort through all those pages to find the page I want. Instead, I can now click on my "Newspaper" group of tabs and it opens 11 tabs at one time. Then I can search the real estate classified section of all these newspapers in about 15 minutes. Figure 5.1 is a screen shot of my browser with the newspaper groups open.

You need to go to www.Mozilla.com and download the latest version of Firefox. Once you download and install that program, you can start building your bookmarked pages for tabbed browsing. Internet Explorer's latest version also offers tabbed browsing. However, I like Firefox better because it has many more features. You can create bookmarks with tabbed browsing in the latest version of Internet Explorer just as well.

You can do this for the types of web sites that you refer to frequently like realtors, auctions, bank-owned properties, free online classifieds, rehab contractors, home inspectors, appraisers, property insurance, property managers, accountants, real estate attorneys, houses for sale, investor web sites, houses for rent, newspapers, outsource labor, people finder, REIA clubs, unsecured lines of credit, title companies, and more.

Next, you need to create a set of bookmarks that are customized to your local market. Set up your bookmark categories, newspapers, realtors, free online classifieds, and so on. As you search the Internet and locate valuable sites in each of your categories, bookmark it and add it to the tabs in one of your categories before you leave the site. If it doesn't fit, set up a new category and put it there. I have actually created a complete set of ready-made, customizable bookmarks that I call my Ultimate Internet Search System. It took me 14 months to create and is a part of my *Ultimate Buying Machine!* course, and you can find out more about that at www.UltimateBuyingMachine.com.

ANSWERING SERVICES AND CALL CAPTURE SERVICES TO HANDLE YOUR INCOMING PHONE CALLS

With all of our marketing efforts, whether we're advertising for buyers or sellers, we use a toll-free number that is directed to an answering service.

Marketing, as I mentioned before, is basically anything that makes the phones ring. Once you start marketing, your phone will be ringing off the hook. While it might be educational for you to handle a few calls in the beginning, you won't want to do it for long. And from a time management point of view, I don't recommend it. You're simply wasting your time if you answer every single phone call that comes in as a result of your marketing campaigns. It will wear you down and distract you from the main

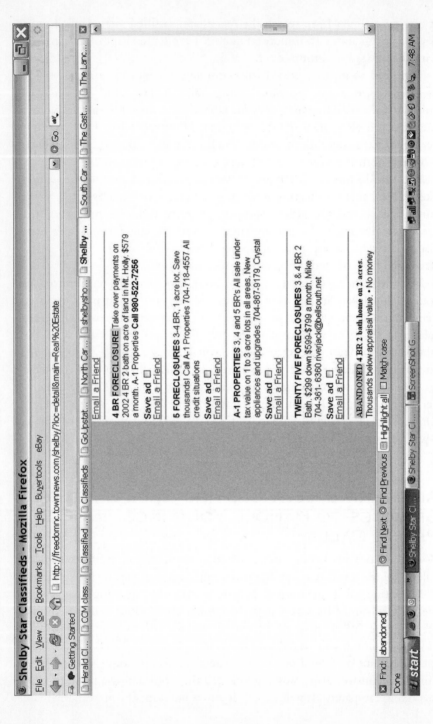

FIGURE 5.1 Newspaper Groups Screen Shot

thing you should be doing—making offers and closing deals. That's how you make money in this business, not wasting your time talking to people who may or may not be good prospects.

You must spend your time talking to prospects. And don't waste a moment on suspects. You can use an answering service or call capture service to sort out the prospects from the suspects. That way, you will know whether you should call them back or not. If you can't reach them, you can put them in your database for follow-up autoresponder e-mail messages and call back at a later time. Then you can spend your time talking to sellers and realtors who have profitable deals that you can make money on.

I used to have all the buyers and sellers call me on my cell phone. I'm very busy. Most of the people who called could never reach me on the first call and had to leave me a message. I would call them back, leave them a message, and they would call me back and leave me message. Finally we would talk. Then five minutes into the conversation, I would discover that the house was not worth my time. One time after playing phone tag, a guy finally told me that his house was valued at $150,000, he owed $145,000, he was current on his payments, and he was in no hurry to sell. All those back-and-forth phone calls were a huge waste of time.

You want to talk to buyers and sellers when you are ready to talk to them. You want to be focused on their deal and be prepared to talk about it. You want to talk to only those people who have a deal that's worth talking about because it could make you money. You want to sort out the suspects from the prospects.

The best way to do this is to have an answering service or a call capture service take the calls for you. These services prescreen callers by getting answers to the important questions before you spend your precious time talking to them. This is especially important if you still have a full- or part-time job.

The biggest difference between the two is that with the answering service, the caller always speaks to a live person instead of leaving voice mail. With call capture, the caller's phone number is always captured whether they leave a message or not. With call capture, you record messages in your own voice, and you can set up multiple mailboxes that give the caller options when they call.

Answering Service

The main benefit of an answering service is that the caller gets to talk to a live person. You get fewer hang ups than you do when using a call capture service. The main drawback of some answering services is that they put people on hold. You should monitor your answering service to make sure they are not putting people on hold. If they put people on hold, they are losing a lot of business for you. Find an answering service that will service your callers immediately and treat them politely. A bad service could alienate a lot of your potential customers, both buyers and sellers.

Because you are buying and selling, you can give the answering service multiple scripts for each type of call. You need to have the service e-mail the calls to you as they come in. This is very important. Remember that until they get you on the phone, they will continue looking for someone to help them. If the caller is a prospect, not just a suspect, then you need to call them back right away. Build rapport and get the caller to like and trust you first, and then you can talk about how you can help them. I like to ask the caller, "How can I help you?" This puts you in a position of them trying to sell you instead of the other way around.

The answering service script asks key questions that will give you the information you are looking for first. For buyers, you want your answering service to discover if they want to buy houses in need of repair, if they have all cash, and if they are willing to close in 10 days. You also want the service to collect all contact information: names, addresses, telephone numbers, fax numbers, and e-mail addresses. If you have a house for sale, you could have the answering service tell callers about the house, its size, the estimated cost of repairs, the after-repair value, your asking price, and the address. Then, if they are interested, they can go take a look at it. You could also ask buyers if they are ready to buy a house in the next 30, 60, or 90 days.

Then the answering service will e-mail your messages to your e-mail inbox as they come in. The information will help sort out the ones you want to call back immediately. Then when you spend time returning calls, building rapport, and getting them to like and trust you, your time and effort will be well spent. You don't need to immediately call back the prospects who tell you they are interested buying a house in 60 or 90 days. You can set them up for a call back later. You can put them all into your database to automatically receive your follow-up messages.

Call Capture Service

Call capture is basically a very sophisticated voice mail system that captures the caller's phone number when they call. It works even for nonpublished and caller-ID blocked numbers. The other great thing is that you can set up multiple mailboxes to handle calls from both sellers and buyers. For example, your message could say, "If you are calling about a house you have for sale please press 1. If you are calling about a home you saw for sale, please press 2." Notice that I use the word house when I'm buying and home when I'm selling. The reason for this is that subliminally a home has more value than a house. Have you ever heard someone say, "There's no place like house"? I don't think so.

Your call capture scripts will be organized in a similar way to your answering service script. The difference is that you will need to organize your questions as a series of options they can choose. You're probably familiar with the way this works. You create a greeting that tells them who you are. You say you sell houses in need of repair to investors at rock-bottom prices. You buy and sell 10 to 15 houses a month and have lots of good deals. You have a great deal now where investors can have 30 percent equity in the house after repairs. All houses are offered with rehab contractor repair estimates and certified appraisals of after-repair value, plus assistance with hard money financing.

At the end of the greeting, you could also give callers an option. For example, "If you are looking for a house in the next 30 days, for all cash, and are willing to close in 10 days, press 1. All others, press 2."

If they press 1, tell them about the house, its size, the estimated cost of repairs, the after-repair value, your asking price, and the address. Ask them to press 1 again and leave their name, address, telephone number, and e-mail address, so that you can put them in your database to receive notifications and announcements from your company. Also tell them that you will call them back.

After they leave their contact information, record another message that thanks them for the call and tells them that someone will return their call shortly.

If they press 2, tell them about the house, its size, the estimated cost of repairs, the after-repair value, your asking price, and the address. Ask them to press 1 and leave their name, address, telephone number, and e-mail address, so that you can put them in your database to receive notifications and announcements from your company.

After they leave their contact information, record an automatic message that thanks them for the call. Then at the end of the message tell them that if they are interested in this house and they can do an all-cash closing in 10 days to press 1. Or press 2 if they are not ready to close in 10 days. Some call capture systems will e-mail you a message whenever someone records a message in your voice mail box. You can call the voice mail box to get your messages. If you get a lot of messages, you can hire someone to call the voice mail box, retrieve the messages for you, transcribe them, and send them to you by e-mail. These are just a few examples of what you could do with a call capture service.

Some people will hang up before leaving a message. But the system will capture their telephone number for you to call back. You can call them back, after you get comfortable with it and start closing deals, or you can hire an outbound service to call these callers back and talk to them personally, getting the required information, and finding out if they are prospects or not.

Some people will not give you all the information. But if they press option number 1, you'll know that they have cash and are willing to close in 10 days. What else do you need to know? Anyone who presses 1 is a great prospect. You will already have their telephone number from the call capture service. Call them back.

There are hundreds of call capture services. We have had success using www.FreedomVoice.com.

VANITY NUMBERS

If you can, you need to get a vanity number. A vanity number is like 1-877-LarryGo. (This is a real number.) There are two ways to go about it. You can get a new number that matches the words you want to use. You can also check to see if your current number has any possible words to use and also check the numbers for certain words at www.Phonetic.com.

Next, I'll tell you how to uncover motivated sellers who will sell you their houses at below-market prices. Remember that when we first find a property, it is not a deal and we have to negotiate it to make it a deal. Deals are made, not found.

CHAPTER 6

FIND MOTIVATED SELLERS—CHERRY-PICK THE HOTTEST BARGAINS AT BELOW WHOLESALE PRICES

Once you have your database of hungry motivated buyers in place, then you have to find houses to supply them. You know exactly the kind of houses, the price range, and the locations of these houses. Now you want to set in motion a steady flow of motivated sellers to supply you with houses at below wholesale prices.

At first glance, these are not readily apparent. Most of the ads you see are for houses that are being sold at full price. You are wasting your time if you try to get every seller to lower his or her price to the level you need to make money. If you spend your time going after all of them, you're in for a lot of disappointment.

You are mainly looking for distressed sellers. You must only deal with motivated sellers and not waste your time dealing with unmotivated sellers. What's the difference? Motivated sellers have to sell. Unmotivated sellers want to sell.

Most sellers are unmotivated. They've put a lot of time and money into maintaining and fixing up their houses. When they sell, they want to get top dollar and not a penny less. They are tough to negotiate with because they have the time and money to hold out for the best price. I don't blame them. I would do the same thing. But I don't want to waste my time trying to negotiate with them. Neither should you. You can't turn an unmotivated seller into a motivated one.

Motivated sellers are the homeowners who are in dire straits. In most cases, some unexpected event in life has led them into financial difficulty: Medical problems, loss of job, business reversal, or a death in the family can result in a situation where they need to sell. Sometimes there's a problem with the house: Flooding, termites, foundation problems, roof problems, fire, or hurricane damage can catch a homeowner without adequate funds to handle it. Sometimes a life transition, job transfer, downsizing to a smaller place, or divorce can force a homeowner to sell. It can happen to anyone. My advice is to treat everyone with respect and compassion no matter what their situation.

Frustrated landlords and investors are also a good source of motivated sellers. Lots of investors have houses they don't have the money to fix up and sell. They made a bad deal, they lost their financing, they took on more problems than they could handle. It happens every day. You can help them by buying their problem house from them, at a steep discount. They are fed up and extremely motivated.

The same goes for landlords. Many are tired of dealing with tenants, sick of the squabbles, fed up with tenants' complaints and petty grievances, and weary of having to chase down delinquent rent payments. In this category, you're likely to find sellers who are excited by your offer and willing to give it their serious consideration.

You can usually find motivated sellers wherever you find vacant houses, houses in need of repair, foreclosures, estate sales, probate, code violations, preforeclosures, divorces, out of towners, heirs, houses with delinquent taxes, condemned houses, bank-owned houses, homeowners who moved to a new home and need to sell their previous homes, and more.

Some of these properties will be listed, and you can buy them through a realtor. Some of them will be for sale by owners (FSBOs). Some will be homeowners who have given up or who don't think anyone would buy their house; so they are not actively engaged in the selling process.

Building a database of motivated sellers is similar to developing your buyers list. Finding sellers mainly involves marketing so that they come to you, networking with personal contacts, and prospecting where you approach them. Again, you can do all three methods online and offline.

Try these methods in your local area and see what works best for you. In some areas, you may work with realtors to get a lot of properties, and in other areas, you may focus on tracking down the owners of vacant houses. It will just depend on your specific area and the market. This is something only you will be able to determine after doing some research by asking the investors you meet how they get their properties and also asking all the realtors you talk to about the market and if they work with many investors, and so on.

MARKETING

I would rather have 10 ways to get one lead than one way to get 10 leads. That is very important. If you are only relying on one source, you are not going to get very many calls. Next you will find many different methods and ways to locate deals and generate leads. Some you have heard before, but I am sure there are some here that you have not. You will not use all of these ideas, but you do need to keep 5 to 10 different ways going at a time in order to keep enough leads coming in.

You don't have to spend a lot of money to market your day trading business. I don't. I recently interviewed a person who was interested in coming to work with us. On interviews, I let at least one of the other team members sit in to see if they think the person will fit in. During this interview the applicant asked, "What is your marketing budget?" We just looked at each other and laughed and said "It's zero! We don't have a marketing budget." So you really can get started without any out-of-pocket expense for marketing.

Co-Op Advertising

This is the best way to start marketing if you have *zero* marketing budget. Using co-op advertising, you can start any type of marketing campaign with absolutely no cash or credit. Yes, you can get all of your marketing for free. Although it will take a little effort on your part, once you set this up, you will be able to run your campaigns 100 percent cost free.

Here is how it works: Contact any business that would like to market in certain neighborhoods or to homeowners specifically and have them place an ad on your marketing piece. You can do this with postcards, flyers, direct mail letters, door hangers, and more. There are many types of businesses that you could co-op with including: mortgage company, realtor, home improvement company, restaurants that deliver, pizza restaurant, landscaper, credit repair company, appraiser, furniture business, furniture rental center, car dealer, and so on.

Just think of any business in your area that you have seen advertise in the paper or anywhere else and contact the owner about your co-op advertising opportunity. If they will run one ad, they will run another one with you. Now if you are not very good at designing an ad, postcard, flyer, and so on, here is a source you can use on a need-to basis. Go to www.elance.com or www.workaholicsforhire.com and post your project, then professionals will bid on your project. You will probably pay between $20 to $40 dollars to have a flyer or postcard designed. You could even get your co-op advertiser to pay for that, too. We use them all of the time for lots of things.

I realize that doing a co-op may take a little effort, but it is absolutely a great way for you to start marketing with no cash or credit. Even after you get some cash, you already have your co-op relationships established, so it is just as easy to continue doing it as it would be to go it alone.

Bandit Signs

Bandit signs are the least expensive and most effective form of marketing. These are the little 18-by-24- or 12-by-18-inch signs that you see on the side of the road or on telephone poles and trees. My sign is very simple—yellow with black letters. The colors yellow and black signify budget or economy. My signs stand out and get a lot of attention from people driving by or waiting at stoplights. Make yours simple so that people can read them easily. Think of them as small billboards. You've got to make your message bold and clear. You shouldn't have a lot of information on the sign. We used to have a sign that said, "I buy houses, any condition, any situation, any price, 1-800-XXX-XXXX." That is too much information. A person in a car at an intersection, going down the road, or looking at the front of one of your houses cannot read all of that. So keep it simple. Ours simply says, "I buy houses, 1-800-XXX-XXXX."

In many areas, bandit signs are illegal. You should really put them on wire holders, like the political signs that pop up every year around election time. But many people illegally put them on telephone poles, which could net you a call from the local code enforcement officer. If and when you get a call from a code enforcement officer advising you about your signs, here's a way to turn it into a buying opportunity.

First, agree with them and let them know you will take the signs down as soon as possible; however, while on the phone with them, tell them that, as they can see, you buy houses. Then ask them if they ever have any properties under code enforcement that either they can't find the owner of or they can't get the owner to repair. Offer to help them by giving you the information. Remember, this is public information so they are not doing anything wrong by telling you about a property under code enforcement. I have built strong relationships that all started with code enforcement officers calling to tell me to take my signs down. Now that's how you turn lemons into lemonade! I'm not suggesting that you do anything illegal, so check your local laws before putting up any signs.

There are many places where you can put out signs. In fact, not only can you put them out on stands near the road, on the highway, or in front of property that you have, but I actually have a couple of businesses that I have given my signs to and they put them in their windows and then I either pay them rent, a commission on a property I buy, or I pay them per lead. There is an endless number of the types of businesses you can do this with. Just keep some signs in your car and stop by one or two businesses each day to ask the owner if you can put your sign in his or her window. As an example, I displayed one of my signs in a local auto repair shop, the owner has sent me several leads, and one of them closed. I purchased the property for $80,000 and sold it for $100,000. The person I sold it to put $7,000 in it and sold it retail for $139,000. Now that's a win-win transaction.

In North Carolina where I do some of my business, you cannot pay a person a referral fee for an actual transaction, but you can pay them for that lead. So just be careful and know your state laws, whether you pay them a referral fee or a lead fee. A lead fee would be okay; that is just like buying leads. If you are in a state where they do not allow paying referral fees, the Real Estate Commission considers that like operating as a Realtor without a license, then you have to pay per lead. But don't ever try to do something that is going to get you in trouble. It will just shut you down and give you a bad reputation. Check with the leaders of your local real estate investors association or contact the state real estate commission to find out your state's laws.

My area has lots of new home communities, and sign placement companies put out all the open house signs and new home community signs for the builders on Friday and then come and pick them up every Monday morning. If you have sign placement companies in your area, you could hire them to put your "I Buy Houses" signs out right along with the new home signs. Think about it. Many people who want to buy a new home already have another one they need to sell first, so you are probably the first one they will call because your sign caught them at the exact time they were looking to buy a new home. When you see all the new home signs out together then call one of the numbers listed and ask who puts them out. Then you can contact that company or individual to put your signs out, too.

How about putting your signs out near retirement homes and communities? Many people going to the community or retirement homes will see your signs, and some of them may have property they need to sell.

Hire Others to Do the Grunt Work   When putting out signs in different areas, I do not put them out myself. I hire somebody to do it—a college student, your teenager, a neighbor's teenager, and so on. You could even contact your church or other churches locally to ask if they know of someone who needs some work or to see if you could get the church's youth group to put them out in exchange for you making a donation to the youth group. Be sure to check out liability issues first because you do not want to be responsible if someone gets hurt.

I pay $2 per sign, and they have to bring me pictures of all the signs they have placed, which is included in the $2. The picture is just a quality control measure. I don't really need the picture, I just want to make sure they are not going out and throwing them in a dumpster and coming back to collect their $2 per sign.

Here's a way to get *free* sign stands for an entire year. Every year right after the local elections, call your local campaign headquarters and offer to help take their signs up for free if you can keep the stands. This is a great source.

We used to put out about 100 to 300 signs every month. However, with all the other automated online marketing we do now, we do not put out many signs anymore.

Business Cards

You can distribute large quantities of your business cards. It's a very economical marketing tool that can bring you lots of phone calls and leads. Give them out to waitresses, at gas stations, at the store, wherever you are or go. Make sure your business card says something very simple. It's as simple as saying, "I Buy Houses," and giving them your phone number to call. Once you get a lot of them out there, you'll get lots of calls.

I sometimes wear a flashing name tag that reads "I Buy Houses. . . . Ask Me." This really works. One day a student of mine who was wearing a similar flashing name tag was in Wal-Mart and someone came up to him who was in town for only a few days to settle an estate, and the student went to look at the property, worked the deal out on the spot, and purchased it. You can get flashing name tags at www.streettags.com.

If you have a card like the million-dollar-bill business card that I use, you can put them anywhere, and I promise you, they will be gone the next day. We have a restaurant in Lake Wylie where I live, and every time I go in, I put down a handful of my million-dollar-bill business cards. I have gone back the very next day, and every one of them is gone.

My million-dollar-bill business card has been a good door opener for me. One of my rental properties was located on a deadend street with no traffic. I went up to the house on the corner, knocked on the door, and I told the lady I had a house down the street that I was looking to rent. I explained that I had no place to put a sign and asked her if she would help. I told her that if she would allow me to put one of my "for rent" or "rent to own" signs in her yard with an arrow pointing down the street, I would give her a million dollars. So I handed her my million-dollar-bill business card. Her eyes lit up, and a big smile came across her face as she looked at it. We both had a good laugh. I put the sign in her yard as she watched, smiling. That's how to use your business card as a door opener.

Magnetic Business Cards   If you have magnetic business cards, you can put them on vending machines, gas pumps, anything metal where lots of people pass by each day. This is a great way to get your name out to the public. What if every time you go to Home Depot you put some magnetic business cards on the vending machines? You can put them into envelopes when you are doing a mailing, and the recipients can keep them and put them on their refrigerators. You can also give them out or put them anywhere you would normally put a business card or flyer.

Here is another unique idea of something to do with them. You can put magnetic signs on your vehicle saying that you buy houses, then put about 10 of these magnetic cards on your vehicle so that when someone sees your vehicle sign in a parking lot, they can just come up to the vehicle and grab one of your cards. This is an awesome idea, and it works!

The Big Business Card   A friend of mine was out of business cards, so he took one of his 12-by-18-inch bandit signs into the office of a realtor he was visiting. I thought that was a great idea. So I printed up some big business cards and started handing them out to realtors. Wow! Did that get a lot of attention.

I actually had signs made that look like business cards. I made them 8 inches by 10 inches so they would fit into an envelope with a cover letter. Your big business card should say that you buy houses and include your name, phone number, and other contact information. Every time you go into the office of people in the real estate business like, appraisers, mortgage brokers, contractors, building inspectors, realtors, investors, and property management companies, you can give them your big business card and tell them to hang it on the wall. This helps them remember you, and they will call you before they call anybody else. And once they hang it on the wall,

all of the other agents and employees in their office will see your business card and that will give you even more exposure.

Next, you can use a sample letter to mail out your big business cards to realtors to get even more and better exposure. It is best to mail the letter and big business card to realtors you have talked to first on the phone. It is expensive to mail. Make sure that you only mail it to professional realtors who are active full time in the business.

Read the letter in Figure 6.1 carefully because it explains my strategy for dealing with realtors and owners/sellers. In the letter, I show how I am different from many of the other investors they might have dealt with before. I stand out from the crowd because before we get off the phone, I will make an offer with minimal stipulations, all cash closings, no financing contingencies, and I purchase most of my properties from realtors. This is a winning proposition for realtors and will ensure their favorable attention.

Flyers

The next thing you want to use to promote your business is flyers. One of the key things about flyers is that you don't want to waste any part of the flyer. If you are buying houses, put that on one side, and if you are also selling houses, put that on the other side. Where can you display them? You can put them at Laundromats, convenience stores, gas stations, or wherever there is a lot of traffic.

You can use sources like Valpak, Advo, grocery store inserts, or you can contact a newspaper and ask about inserting a flyer in the next delivery. You can also look in your local Sunday paper at all the sale papers. The contact information of who publishes the advertisements in the sales circulars usually appears along the edges of the sheet. Contact them and see how much it will cost to get your flyer into their insert with all the other national advertisers. You can target certain areas and certain regions, which is pretty good.

Be a little creative with flyers. Use fluorescent colors, anything to make your flyer stand out and be unique. Put pictures on it, put a picture of yourself, a picture of a property, but again, be different.

Postcards

Another way you can market your business is through postcards. These are great because they allow you to target your best prospects and get them to call you. There are many different types of postcards. Who can you mail them to? You can mail them to properties that are under code enforcement,

Investors Rehab, Inc.

PO Box 5261
Lake Wylie, SC 29710
Office: 803-831-0056
Fax: 803-831-0805

Dear <Realtor name here>,

My name is <your name here>, and I am a real estate investor. I want to introduce myself to you and send you my business card. (or if you have spoken to them recently and you are following up you can say that as well.)

As you can see by my unique card, I am **NOT** your average investor. My company purchases 10 to 15 houses per month. I have plenty of references I can give you, if you need them. We actually purchase most of our properties from realtors.

If you use a service to send out e-mail notices of available properties, please add me to your list. (then type in here the types of properties you are looking for and your e-mail address.)

Please hang my business card on the wall over your desk so when other agents in the office see it and think of a property that would be a good investment, they will tell you to contact me so we can make an offer. Also, it will remind you of me when you see or think of a good investment.

I will always make an offer on anything that you contact me about before we get off the phone. We have very minimal stipulations and set up all-cash closings with no financing contingencies. Is this WIN-WIN or what?

I NEED MORE HOUSES! Please take a minute to ask around the office and try to think of any problem properties that we can make an offer on today. Let's close some deals and make some money together!

(If you have another business or service place it here)
We also are in the mortgage business and offer traditional, rehab, and hard money loans to investors. We can loan the money to purchase and rehab a property for an investor. Please feel free to visit our website at www.financialhelpservices.com.

Please feel free to contact me any time you have a property that we need to look at or if we can help any of your other investor customers close a deal!

Thank You,

Larry Goins

Copyright © 2009 by Larry Goins. To customize this document, download Figure 6.1 to your hard drive from www.realestatedaytrading.com/bonuses. The document can then be opened, edited, and printed using Microsoft Word or another popular word processing application.

FIGURE 6.1   Sample Letter

in foreclosure, inherited, owned by out of towners, or owned by Section 8 landlords, to name a few. Information about Section 8 properties is public information, which you should be able to get from your city's Public Housing Agency office. Get a mailing list of Section 8 property owners; sometimes these are "don't wanter" landlords. Get a list of the out-of-town owners from the tax assessor's office. You can get a list of foreclosures from any of the many listing services that you can find by doing a Google search for the term "foreclosures."

Use bright colors on your postcards. Make them look personal rather than like a mass-marketing piece. Be sure to use bright colors. Sometimes oversized postcards work very well. The good thing about a postcard is that it is cheaper to mail than a letter. And it is already opened so readership is much higher than with a letter. People will at least look at it. You do not have to worry about whether or not they have opened your mail.

You can have someone at www.elance.com or www.Guru.com create your own postcard for you.

Then all you have to do is get your mailing list printed on labels, slap the labels and stamps on the postcards, and mail them. This can be somewhat expensive, but very effective if you have a responsive list. Try it first in small quantities. Be sure to include a code on the postcards that corresponds to the mailing list you are using. When the calls come in, have your answering service record the codes so that you can track the response. If it works when you test it, then you can order more lists from the same source and expect to get roughly the same response.

Figure 6.2 is a sample of one of our postcards. If you would like to see more samples of my postcards that you can use and edit, you can get one for free by going to www.realestatedaytrading.com and clicking on forms and documents.

Classified Newspaper Ads and Free Online Classifieds

Newspaper classifieds is one of the fastest ways to get a steady stream of interested sellers coming your way. Many people run ads, so you've got to be creative about what you run and where you run it. Run your ads under "houses for sale." Also try running them under "houses for rent." You might even find that you can do better by running a small 1-inch-by-1-column display ad in the general news pages or business pages outside the classifieds. By the way, if you run a display ad, the best place to post your ad is on page three, on the bottom right. This is the first thing people see when they open the newspaper to the first full-page spread page.

Dear Property Owner,

We Buy Houses CA$H!

Do you own an **unwanted home** and **need to sell quickly?** Does your house need repairs? Are you behind on payments? In foreclosure? Relocating? Lost your job? Suffered the loss of a loved one to divorce or death?...

Investors Rehab

THESE PROBLEMS CAN HAPPEN TO ANYONE

**We Buy Houses** in any price range, any area and **any condition.**

We can pay cash or take over your payments to alleviate your debt immediately.

We are not realtors. We are real estate investors who buy several houses per month and can buy yours today! You'll get a quick sale with no hassles.

Leave your worries behind you! There is no cost or obligation so call us today!

Call 1-800-526-3054

P.S. If you are holding more than one unwanted property, please tell us about ALL OF THEM!

FIGURE 6.2   Postcard Sample

In the last few years we've switched to free online classifieds like Craigslist.com, InetGiant.com, FreeAdLists.com, USFreeAds.com, and DomesticSale.com. You can post your e-mail address and phone number, but if you have a web site you can list it as well. Don't do the posting yourself. Outsource this job to a professional. Here's the name of a company that will post your online ads for you: PostingForYou.com. If you do this, you will have an ample supply of motivated sellers coming to you fast.

You can also run a classified ad on eBay to find motivated sellers that you can add to your database. Running an ad for 30 days costs $150, and a 90-day ad costs $300. Be sure to test the ad first to see if it brings in enough sellers to justify the cost.

Here are three samples of different ads we have used in the past, which really worked well for us. They are simple, short, and to the point. The first one is:

I buy houses, apartments, lots, and land. Quick cash. Any condition. Anywhere. Call Larry 1-877-LAR-RYGOins.

Another ad that is good for finding people who are in foreclosure is:

In foreclosure? Save your credit, not a loan. Call Larry—1-877-LAR-RYGOins.

Whenever people facing foreclosure call, have your voice mail message or answering service tell them how you can pay off their loan, save their credit, and give them a little bit of time to move out.

The third ad that I want to share with you is directed to frustrated landlords:

Do you own rentals but are sick of management? I can help. Call Larry—1-877-LAR-RYGOins.

Below is the best ad I have ever used. This is one way to find vacant properties without having to find the vacant property owner first. Direct this ad to owners of houses in the same neighborhood as vacant houses in disrepair.

Is there a house that is bringing down your neighborhood? Trashy, abandoned? I can help. Call Larry—1-877-LAR-RYGOins.

You can also run an ad very inexpensively in your entire state or a region of your state by contacting your state's press association. They usually have three options for advertising:

1. Statewide classifieds
2. Statewide 2-by-2 ads (This is 2 columns wide by 2 inches high.)
3. Press release services (They will send a press release to every newspaper in your state.)

Depending on the state, you may be able to select a region to advertise instead of the entire state. To find your state's press association, I would suggest that you Google "your state press association" (e.g., "North Carolina Press Association").

Vehicle Signs

All businesspeople need to have signs on their cars. My sign used to say: I buy, sell, build, remodel, and finance homes. When I used this sign, I only got a few calls all year. That is because the sign had too many words for people to comprehend. I had to shorten it down to: "I buy houses, 1-800-XXX-XXXX." Now I get a ton of calls.

I also put a license plate frame on my vehicle, which is a scrolling LED that simply reads: I buy houses 1-800-XXX-XXXX. It scrolls across every time I turn my lights on, even the fog lights. You can get license plate frames at www.streettags.com.

Billboards

You have probably seen HomeVester's billboards: "I Buy Ugly Houses" or "Ug Buys Ugly Houses Now." If you plan to use billboards, put them in the low-income areas where the houses you want to buy are located. It is a waste of money putting them in the higher-end areas.

Take One Box

Most people think only about displaying their flyers in take one boxes at the properties they are selling. What about hanging one either on your car door or on the back of your SUV? You could put some of your flyers with "I buy houses" printed on one side and "I sell houses" printed on the other side in the box. Also, because you will already have the "I Buy Houses" magnetic sign on the side of your car, they will know what you do and just come up and get a flyer out of the take one box.

Door Hangers

You can hang door hangers on the doors of properties you have found that are in foreclosure. Be sure to pay people to do this for you because putting them out yourself is not a good use of your time. You could pay one of your rehab guys to have their employees put them out for you. You could even list their company name on the back for them in exchange for them putting the hangers out for you. This is a win-win.

You could do this with many types of businesses. How about approaching a local independent restaurant and paying for the printing with your ad on one side and theirs on the other if they deliver and hang them. You could also do this with a pizza delivery service. You can put an ad on a local independent pizza company's box so everyone who gets a delivery will know about you. In exchange you could provide the boxes. You could also place your ad on restaurant placemats in exchange for printing up the placemats.

Promotional Items

Promotional items can keep your name and your "I Buy Houses" message in front of your potential clients for a long time. The idea here is to find something useful that people will keep and use that displays your name, contact information, and selling message. You can buy just about anything and have your name put on it: pens, calendars, pot holders, sunglasses, shirts, lanyards, and so on. We buy pens and lanyards and give them out at the real estate investors meetings. Members/investors keep our lanyards to hang their membership badges on. You could also work a deal with your investor's club to provide them with a lanyard for each and every new member. What a bargain for both parties. Sometimes, we also provide note pads to hand out at the investor's meetings so that when members take notes they will always have our name in front of them.

Ads on Buses and Bus Benches

If you live in an area where they have public transit, you may consider running an ad on the side of one of the buses. This is a great source with lots of exposure. This also works great in branding your company as well as building your list.

Bus stops have bus benches where you also can run your ads. Thousands of people traveling along these streets every day will see your ad. I know a guy who got a discount by buying an ad on every bus bench in the city. He has a huge presence, and this is really a good source.

Direct Mail

You might get a fabulous response by mailing a personalized letter to a mailing list of motivated sellers. Many investors use direct mail to generate phone calls from sellers. First, you need a list to target.

The best targeted lists of motivated sellers are foreclosures, out-of-town owners, expired listings, bankruptcies, and divorces. Lists of foreclosures are not hard to find. They are all over the Internet. The most popular ones are realtytrac.com, foreclosure.com, and foreclosures.com. To find more, Google "foreclosures" and thousands will come up.

A list of out-of-town owners is a great list because these are people who have houses in your town but live in another town. Some of them are renting the house out to others, and some of them are vacant. Many are in disrepair. Lots of these absentee owners want to get rid of the house but don't have the time or money to get them into a good enough condition to sell. There are two sources for lists of out-of-town owners: realtors and the courthouse tax roles. If you have a realtor friend, he or she might be willing to do this for you. That's why you want to be in the good graces of many realtors. They can be a great help to you. Or you can simply go down to the courthouse and ask a clerk to pull up a list of out-of-town owners for you.

Expired listings are people who have had their house on the market, and the listing expired without the house selling. Not all of them, but some of them are frustrated and motivated sellers, ready to give up on selling their house at full-market price. Some are still hoping to sell for full price and aren't likely to give an inch. For a list of them, check with your realtor friend. Anyone with access to the MLS can pull up a list of expired listings in minutes.

Bankruptcy and divorce lists contain a lot of motivated sellers. These are on public record, and you can find them at your courthouse. You can search your county clerk's office under civil proceedings to find divorces that have been filed. Cases that read Jones versus Jones are often divorces. You can find a listing of bankruptcies at the following web site: http://pacer.psc.uscourts.gov. Bankruptcies are great because when the bankruptcy is final and the property is clear, you often have a seller who is motivated to sell. A lot of states have homeowner's exemptions to protect homeowners from losing their houses in bankruptcy. InfoUSA is a mailing list brokerage that rents mailing lists of bankruptcies and tax liens. You can find them at www.infousa.com.

You can also address your mailings to homeowners in the zip codes where you want to buy houses. You can target the homeowners in your target zip codes by income level. Lower-income homeowners have a greater chance of being motivated sellers. By mailing to this list, you could uncover quite a few motivated sellers. USADATA is another mailing list company that could help you put together the best list for your mailing. Find them at www.usadata.com.

Remember, mailing lists come in a great variety of shapes and forms. Some of them will work for you, and some of them will not. Don't invest in a large expensive mailing without testing your mailing first in small quantities. Start with a 500-name mailing to each list. Code the list with an extension number to track responses and sales. That means the mailing piece you send out should be coded with a phone number, followed by another code number that represents the list you are using. The telephone calls should be received by your call capture service or answering service. As part of the script, your operator should ask callers for the code number on the mail they received.

If you get a high enough response rate then you can order more names from the lists that work and mail in larger quantities. If you find a list that is extremely responsive, then you should go back and mail it a second or third time until the response dwindles off. The timing between each mailing is also an issue. You could try spacing your mailings to the same list a week apart. But that might be too frequent. If response rates drop too much try scheduling the mailings a month or so apart.

Make your communication as personal as possible. Hand addressed envelopes work the best. Use a first-class stamp. Put a return address label with your name and address on it, just like you would do if you were sending a personal letter to a friend. And the letter inside should read as if you are writing to someone you know personally. The letter should be short and handwritten. Just tell them you want to make an offer on their house. And ask them to give you a call. Don't use your company name and don't make it look like a commercial mailing. You'll get lots of calls.

If you don't want to hand address all those letters yourself, I don't blame you. Here are some services that will do it for you: www.thinkinkmarketing.com, www.writeonresults.com, www.tomrichardmarketing.com, and www.fasprint.com.

Google

Adwords   With Google you can run advertising campaigns on Google Adwords. If you go to Google and search for anything, you will see that there are listings down the right side of the page and also one or two at the top with a different background. These are paid advertisements.

You can go to Google and set up an account to run your ad. When the user clicks on your link it will take them to your web site, which will have an offer. What will you offer? As described above, you'll offer a free report of some kind. In this case you want to offer a free report of interest to motivated sellers. For example, one of my reports is called, *Secrets of*

Selling Your House in 7 Days. Once the seeker comes to my web site, I ask them to give me their contact information before they can download the free report. Their contact information is automatically stored in my seller database for future autoresponder messages from me. My autoresponder software automatically sends them *Secrets of Selling Your House in 7 Days.* It's all done without me even lifting a finger.

As I mentioned in the previous chapter, you need to register your domain name and set up a marketing web site. If you do not have a web site, you can get a generic web site very cheap. But remember that you get what you pay for. If you would like to look at a sample of the web site we use to market for leads and sell our properties, you can visit www.UltimateInternetMarketingMachine.com.

You need software to e-mail your report, collect contact information, and add it to your database. The software will also automatically process deletions from your database. 1Shopping Cart and AWeber.com are online services that can do this for you. Our web site also does this for you automatically.

Next, you need to build traffic to your site. That's where pay-per-click advertising services like Google Adwords, Overture, and Yahoo Search Marketing come in. You place a small ad on Google Adwords that comes up when people type a certain search term into Google Search. Maybe sellers who are looking for ways to sell their houses type in "selling home." Then your ad would come up. If it appeals to them they will click on it and go to your web site.

What do you put in the ad? Google restricts the number of characters you may use on each line of the ad. In the Google ad, you want to advertise your free report and attract sellers to visit your site and opt in for your free report and to receive further correspondence from you. Then if you contact them, you won't be accused of spamming them, because by opting in they have agreed to receive your e-mails. Let's say you are offering a free report entitled, *How to Sell Your House in 7 Days in Any Market.*

You must select the keyword the seller will use to search. Your ad will appear whenever the seller searches using that word or phrase. Let's say you select the keyword, "selling home." Then your Google ad might read:

Selling Your Home?

The Fast and Easy Way to Sell Your House.

No Fees. Free Guide.

But if you select the keyword, "stop foreclosure" then your Google ad would be different. It might read:

> Stop Foreclosure
>
> The Secrets To Selling Your Home
>
> Quickly and Easily. Free Guide.

Each of these is considered a separate Adword campaign. You can run more than one ad in each campaign, and you can run as many ad campaigns as you want.

You want your ad to attract only motivated sellers. You don't want people clicking on your ad who are not really interested. In pay-per-click advertising, you pay for every click whether it comes from a good prospect or not. You pay for your ad based on a cost per click. You may bid to pay 5¢ per click or $5 per click. This can get very expensive. It all depends on the keyword you choose and the page ranking you want. Some keywords are in great demand, and the price for those has been bid up to a high level. If you want to get a high page ranking on some keywords you might have to pay $1 to $5 per word. The more in demand the keyword and higher in the page ranking you want, the more expensive the ad. Some ads cost $100 per click.

To reduce the cost, you can also set it up so that your ads will only show up if someone in your area is searching for your particular keywords. If you are in Orlando, Florida, for example, you may only want people who live within 50 miles to see your Google ad. In that case, any time someone who is 50 miles or farther away from you inputs a search, your ad will not appear, which will save you money by preventing people outside of your area from clicking on your ad because that's how you pay.

You also want to be careful when you select your keywords. You want keywords that will attract only motivated sellers. That is why you have to choose keywords that your motivated sellers might use to find someone to buy their house. Use narrow targeted keywords. If you select keywords that are too broad, you will get more people clicking, but many of these will be people who really have a house to sell. But you still have to pay for those clicks.

Here's the link to Google's Adword keyword selection tool: https://adwords.google.com/select/KeywordToolExternal. You can use this tool to find out how many Google searches your keywords get each month.

Carefully test your Adword campaign first on a small scale. Google allows you to put a limit on the amount of money you spend on each campaign per day. The neat thing about Google is that you can set a daily and monthly budget. For example, you can set your daily budget at $5 a day and your monthly budget at $500 if you want. Watch your expenses and don't get carried away. See adwords.google.com for details.

Yahoo Search Marketing has a similar service. For details go to: www.sem.smallbusiness.yahoo.com/searchenginemarketing.

And even FaceBook has entered this marketing arena with their new service, FaceBook Advertising. Go here for details: www.facebook.com/ads.

You can also build traffic to your web site by running free online classifieds, and banner ads on high-traffic real estate sites and in niche market real estate ezines. Once you have all the pieces in place, the sky's the limit!

Adsense   Google Adsense is another type of advertising you can do through Google. Have you ever been to a web site and seen the listing of Google ads down one side or the other and the top of the web page reads: "ads sponsored by Google"? These are Adsense advertisers. You set up your Google campaigns the same way, but you just specify that you want your ad to be shown on other related web sites, not just Google searches. You can still select a geographic area so you aren't wasting money on clicks out of your area.

NETWORKING

Estate Investors Associations

Your local club is a great source of networking for buyers, sellers, rehabbers, appraisers, attorneys, realtors, and property managers. Distribute your "I Buy Houses" business cards with your phone number to everyone you meet and tell them to contact you whenever they have a house to sell. Remind them that you will make an offer on any house before you get off the phone, and you will close with all cash in seven days.

Word-of-Mouth Advertising

This sounds very simple, but don't discount it because it will not work if you don't use it. Tell everyone you meet that you are an investor and you buy property. When you do this, you will be surprised at how many people run into other people who need to sell a property, and if they know you buy property, then you will get the call.

I actually talked to a new investor recently who told me of the three deals he had purchased; the first two came from coworkers. He just told everyone he knew that he started investing. His coworkers told him about someone who they knew who wanted to sell a property. Insider leads like that are the best. It's so easy to call someone and say that a friend of theirs told you to give them a call about a property they have for sale. It's an instant icebreaker.

Bird Dogs

This can be a great way to have people out finding deals for you. This involves finding some new investors who want to get into the business. Ask them to look for deals and send them to you. They are basically your bird dogs pointing out deals for you. The best way to find them is at your local real estate investors association. If you do decide to pursue this method, please make sure you are aware of your state laws on paying commissions to unlicensed people who send you a property. If your state has no laws against it, you could pay them a percentage of every deal you close. If your state doesn't allow this, then you can pay them a lower amount but pay them for every lead whether or not the deal closes. To learn about your state laws, you can contact the real estate commission in your state. To find them, just Google the name of your state along with the words "real estate commission."

PROSPECTING

Prospecting is anything that you do that requires you to dig and search in order to contact the owner or the seller of a property. Prospecting involves calling realtors, conducting online searches, driving the neighborhood looking for vacant houses, or hiring others to drive neighborhoods and bring deals to you.

When you are prospecting, you must know what you are looking for. If you don't, it can be a gigantic time waster. You must very selective and only contact the best prospects, the ones who have houses to sell and are desperate. These are the contacts that can boost your income.

Look for the Gap

Unless you are working a preforeclosure to do a short sale, look for deals that have a little bit of margin already. If the asking price is below the market value, you know you have a motivated seller. You're looking for gaps between the market price and the asking price. For example, if a 1,200-square-foot, three-bedroom, two-bath house in a certain neighborhood is selling for $120,000, and your prospect is already asking $95,000, you have a gap. And there is a good possibility that seller will go even lower in price. I would call about it.

If there is a house on the market, and it is worth $105,000, and the owner is asking $105,900, then I would not even look at that house because there is no gap. However, if the seller is behind on the mortgage, then he or she is definitely motivated. A short sale is possible, so I may want to call about that property.

You should also look for vacant houses, houses in disrepair, houses with absentee owners, in probate, with tax liens, in divorce, and generally, any houses where the owner is in distress.

In this section, I'll give you a lot of information about locating properties and finding deals. But remember, in reality it is very, very, very rare that you actually find a deal. Deals are made, not found. You have to make your own deals by building rapport, getting people to like and trust you, and getting to know them. Every time a seller tells you something, make a note of it. Maybe your seller likes to golf, ski, fly fish, or has a child on the Little League baseball team. Write it down or make a mental note. Later when talking to him, you can ask him about his children or favorite hobby. Show you care about your sellers as people and they will trust you more.

There are many different ways to prospect. I am going to share many of them with you. You are not going to use all of them, but I wanted to share enough of them with you so that you can have several different sources out there to get leads and prospects to be able to buy property. For the complete scripts we use for sellers and realtors just go to www.RealEstateDayTrading.com/Bonuses.

Houses Already on the Market

Realtors A realtor who deals with damaged, delinquent, and bank-owned properties could be your best friend and ally for finding motivated sellers. I actually used to buy most of my properties from realtors. Remember, at the beginning of this book, I said to go after the low-hanging fruit in your area. That is what works best and easiest in your market. At one time, realtors were the easiest way in my market, but now, although we buy a lot from realtors, we also use other methods.

Every time you talk to a realtor, get their e-mail address to put in your database. And always ask realtors if they can sign you up for automatic e-mail notification when any properties come on the market that meet your buying criteria. This is very important and can save you a lot of legwork.

Ask them to set it up based on certain keywords, if they can. If so, give them the types of property you are interested in and also a list of keywords. Keywords like motivated, vacant, abandoned, short sale, transferred, bank-owned, handyman special, TLC, needs work, fixer upper, reduced, must sell, bring all offers, and so on. Be sure to call the realtor who sent you the deal and put your offer in through them so that they get their fee if the deal closes. If you find a property on your own while driving or searching the Internet, then go through the listing agent on that property.

Ask realtors to refer sellers they cannot help to you. This mainly applies to sellers in default or foreclosure where there is not enough time to put the property on the market. Tell realtors that you buy houses, pay all cash, and can close in a week. You can help sellers get out of those houses quickly.

In exchange, offer to send the realtor any sellers who you cannot help, which may be a good listing prospect for the realtor. Always try to create win-win situations that benefit all parties. When talking to realtors, be sure to always inquire about pocket listings. These are listings that they may have just acquired, that are not yet listed in the MLS system. If you have a relationship with the realtor, you want them to call you first.

Ask your realtors for reports of expired listings monthly. These are the properties that were on the market but didn't sell. This is a great source of motivated sellers as I mentioned previously when discussing direct mail.

Find the Best REO Realtor in Your Area   Some realtors specialize in real estate owned (REO) or bank-owned properties. These banks are supermotivated and want to get these properties off their books as fast as possible. You can make some great deals. It's important that you find out who the REO realtors are in your area. These are the realtors who work directly with the asset managers or banks that have taken property by foreclosure. Asset managers help banks dispose of these properties.

Ask one of your realtors to send you an e-mail or print you a list of the properties that have already sold with the keywords REO, bank-owned, seller addendum required, and foreclosure. The listing agents of these properties are the realtors who work with the banks and asset managers. They are the ones getting all the foreclosure listings. Get on their e-mail lists, put them on yours, visit their web sites, add them to your bookmarks, and make some offers through them!

Find the Best Realtors in Your Market   You want to find the best realtors by volume of transactions in your area. Don't search for dollar volume because that will favor realtors who sell in high-priced areas, which you don't want. You want the highest number of transactions.

Contact your local realtors association and ask them for the information. Tell them that you want the names of the top five agents by transaction volume. They keep statistics on all of the realtors and properties. You can also get information on the number of properties sold, the median price of the properties that have sold, and ones that are on the market now. Look for the realtors selling the most houses in your target areas. Call them, put them in your database, and get on theirs. The reason you do this is because you want to know which realtors are doing the most business. They are usually the ones who have the most listings, although not always.

Online Searches   We do a lot of Internet searching. Searching online is how we get a large percent of our properties right now. The Internet offers tremendous sources for finding property. As I explained in the last chapter, you can bookmark and tab the most important sites for Internet searching.

This way you can search them very rapidly. This is what I do: set up folders in your bookmarks for each of the different categories of searches, newspapers, free classifieds, bank-owned property, realtor sites, eBay real estate, and auctions sites. I have them all tabbed for quick browsing. Use search engines to find more sites to add to your search categories as you go along.

When scanning ads and listings for prospects, I look for words like: motivated seller, must sell, bank-owned, for investors, needs some work, fire damage, owner leaving town, owner transferred, or best offer (obo), divorce, owner financing, no or low down payment, owner flexible, below appraisal, investor special, handyman special, fixer upper, lease option, rent with option, take up payments, owner desperate, or any other words that signal that this is not a homeowner trying to sell their house at full-market price.

You also want to look for out-of-town phone numbers. When searching the classifieds in Firefox or Internet Explorer, you can highlight the keywords making it easy to find the ads you want to read.

Make sure that every property you consider buying has a picture. Never look at a property without a picture. We just don't have time to waste time on houses without pictures. We are too busy buying 10 to 15 properties and making 40 or 50 offers to stop and track down houses without pictures.

We don't have time to research and get involved in a house if we don't even have any idea of what it looks like.

Keep Track of Properties You Find Online   There are a couple different ways you can keep track of the properties you find online. The first way is to simply set up a group in your bookmarks called "My Properties." Then for every property you find online, you can save the web page in that group.

You can also separate them into different groups based on where the property is located. For example, "My Atlanta Properties" and "My Charlotte Properties." Then when you need to find a promising property that you found online, you can go to your bookmarks and see where you saved it.

You could also create a word document for properties you find online as you are searching. When you come across an ad or listing that appears to be a motivated seller, copy and paste all the information into a file labeled by location and date of search. Paste the whole listing including the picture and the links to the listing page into the word file. Later, you can use this file to make your phone calls, to get information from sellers, and make offers. I also like to place notes below the information so that I can keep up with my offers and the seller's circumstances.

This is the easiest way to keep up with properties that you are looking at right now. You can use this system for all the houses you find, both online and offline. I save listings from realtors, FSBOs, newspapers, and everywhere else. This is an enormous time saver because all the properties I am interested in or have made offers on are all together in one location and I can add notes as I progress into the deal.

Major Web Sites

Newspaper Classifieds   We have about 10 or 11 different newspapers in our surrounding area that we search. I have bookmarks saved to the Real Estate section of the Classifieds, and in about 15 minutes, I can search all the newspapers for "Real Estate for Sale." But I don't just look in that section, I also look under "Real Estate for Rent." Many landlords who are renting property are tired and aggravated and may be ready to sell if a credible buyer like you comes along.

In looking for classifieds, some newspapers use a source like www.abracat.com as their classified search service. You can look there for a local newspapers in your area.

Another thing to keep in mind is that some people do not know if Saturday or Sunday is your real estate day. For example, some people do not know that Saturday is the real estate day in my area and they think Sunday is the best day to run the ads. So always look in the Sunday edition as well, when you are looking either in the physical paper or online.

If your local area has a legal newspaper or a legal section of your newspaper, that can be a potential source. You should look for newly filed Foreclosures or Judgments. Sometimes there are classified ads in there. Divorce listings may be another source.

Free Online Classifieds   I do the same thing for free online classified sites. There are dozens of free online sites that have real estate for sale listings. Here are a few classified sites to add to your bookmarks: Craigslist.com, InetGiant.com, FreeAdLists.com, USFreeAds.com, and DomesticSale.com. Just do a Google search with the keywords "Free online classifieds" to find more.

eBay Real Estate   Also be sure to search and bookmark eBay's real estate site: realestate.ebay.com.

Real Estate for Sale Magazines   The *Real Estate Book* and *Homes and Land* are also good sources. You can search their listings online and also get a free subscription. You can find them at www.RealEstateBook.com and www.HomesAndLand.com.

Real Estate Auctions   Create a folder in your bookmarks for real estate auctions. Many of the properties listed on auction web sites are distressed properties, where the owner is extremely motivated to sell; look for keywords that indicate this motivation. Also look for houses in need of a lot of repairs, possibly with absentee owners. Get the information you need, do an instant property analysis, and make an offer. Some of these properties have few bidders, and you can pick them up real cheap.

Here are some auctions sites to add to your bookmarks under the category auctions: www.proxibid.com, www.auctioneers.org, www.hudsonandmarshall.com, and www.realtybid.com. You'll find more by searching "real estate auctions" with your city name.

Also, I want to suggest that you learn who all the local auction companies are, get on their physical mailing lists as well as their e-mail lists, and call them on a regular basis. Send them your business card, send them a flyer, let them know what you do, and search their web sites often for properties that may be coming up for auction.

Realtor Listings   No need to call your realtor to look up properties for you. Now you can search realtor sites for properties that match your criteria. Add this realtor site to your bookmarks and search it frequently: www.realtor.com.

Bank-Owned Property   We get some of our best deals buying bank-owned property. The banks call them real estate owned or REO. Many banks have to take houses back from homeowners. REOs held on a bank's balance sheet are considered nonperforming assets. Banks don't like them. They wreak havoc on their balance sheets. They don't have the expertise to sell houses and are not set up to do the rehab work necessary to sell them for full price. We get some of our best deals from bank-owned houses. Search these sites regularly and add them to your bookmarks: www .resales.usda.gov, www.mlnusa.com/realestate/listings.asp, www.mcbreo .com, www.buybankhomes.com, www.chase.com, www.bankofamerica .reo.com, www.pasreo.com, www.ocwen.com, and www.nrba.com.

Build Your Bookmarks

Google Searches   Google has a reputation of being the top choice for those searching the Web. Use Google to search with the keywords I listed previously and add your own state or city to find local real estate. You'll get a lot of real estate sites and a lot of realtor sites. Search them for motivated sellers and add them to your bookmarks, tabbing them for future browsing by category. Use Google and other search engines to locate online listings and build your bookmarked categories. Use every major search engine, not just Google.

Also use Yahoo. You'll get excellent search results from Yahoo.com that provides crawler-based listings like Google. You can search the original human-compiled Yahoo! Directory by using the Yahoo! Directory home page as opposed to using the regular Yahoo.com home page.

Broaden your searches further by using: Ask.com. HotBot.com is a good way to search all three of the major search engines: Google, Yahoo! and Ask results all in one search.

If you are an AOL user, you can use the internal version of AOL search that provides links to sites that are only available within AOL.

Google Alerts Google Alerts is a *free* service provided by Google that allows you to list certain keywords of interest to you. Then when something is posted to the Internet related to those keywords, Google will send you an e-mail with a link to the page.

As a real estate day trader, you could use Google Alerts to get notifications about houses for sale that are of interest to you. You could set up an alert with your city or county name plus keywords you use in searching for a property. Here are a few examples: "Charlotte Fixer Upper," "Charlotte handyman special," "Charlotte foreclosure," "Charlotte vacant," "Charlotte abandoned," "Charlotte reduced," "Charlotte must sell," and "Charlotte motivated seller." The list could go on and on.

Houses about to Hit the Market

Houses listed for sale are only the tip of the iceberg. There is a huge, hidden, untapped market of houses that are owned by motivated sellers that are not on the market, not advertised. The owners have given up or are not actively looking to sell. Maybe they don't believe anyone would buy their property in its present condition, and they don't have money to rehab and sell the property at a profit themselves. Here are some of the many sources of unadvertised properties.

Property Managers Property managers know a lot of investors who may have properties to sell. Some are realtors as well as property managers. They give their best leads to clients whose property they are managing. They want to deal with investors who are loyal. The last thing a property manager wants to do is to find a deal, send it to you, and find out that you are going to manage it yourself. It is a good source for property, but you must always let them manage the property you buy, even if you are selling it off in one day to another investor. Get your investor/buyer to agree to let them do the property management at least until the current tenant moves out.

Courthouse Search Courthouses have information on divorces, foreclosures, delinquent property taxes, and out-of-town owners. These are some of the best sources of motivated sellers.

Divorce You look for same last names of male and female in the Book of Civil Lawsuits in the Circuit Court. If they are going through a divorce and they have real property, chances are they are going to sell it. What you may want to do is either call or send them a postcard or letter and put them in your database.

Foreclosures   You can find newly filed foreclosures at the courthouse posted on a bulletin board. Usually, the older the mortgage, the more equity the house will have. Sometimes you will see a very low mortgage balance and a lot of times it is a second mortgage. You can call homeowners directly or send them a letter and let them call you as previously described under direct mail.

Delinquent Property Taxes   Contact the tax office for a list of properties with delinquent taxes owed. Some tax offices even publish this information in the newspapers, and once a year, they publish a list of the property taxes that have not been paid.

In my area, there is actually a guy who produces a CD-ROM that contains this type of information. He goes around to the various counties and gets lists of all the properties with taxes that have not been paid. Then he downloads the lists, puts them in a spreadsheet, puts them on a CD-ROM, and then sells them. I have bought his list several times and sent out mailings. I actually ended up buying a couple of properties from it.

Out-of-Town Owners   The tax department will list the owner's mailing address and many times, you can find it online. If owners live out of town now, they might want to sell their house and buy another one closer to where they live. It is not a bad idea to at least try one or two mailings to see if you can find some out-of-town owners who may want to sell. There are also several different services that can do things like this. One of them is Courthouse Retrieval Service and their web address is www.crsdata.net. We subscribe to it, and you can actually do a search for out-of-town owners, print mailing labels, and put the labels right on your postcards. You can also find any county in the United States in any state by going to the National Association of Counties at www.Naco.org.

Here are some other sources for property, and bear in mind that you will not use all of these sources. You may only use a few of them, but I just wanted to give you some different options. You should keep five to ten sources going at a time so you will have a steady source of leads coming in.

Home Inspectors   Many people have their homes inspected before they put them on the market. So, home inspectors may be good sources for deals every now and then. Talk to them and put them in your database to stay in touch.

Senior Citizen Retirement Homes   You can put a sign up on their bulletin board after you get to know the admissions director or marketing director. Homeowners may want to move in to the facility and need to sell their property first. Also, current residents of the retirement home may have visitors who could be another source or motivated buyers. Maybe parents who are residents need to sell some property. If they see your sign, you may be able to buy the property from them.

Garage Sales   This is a good source because many people have garage sales before moving out of town. You can check the papers for them and because most of them are on Saturday, it's a good day to drive the neighborhoods that you want to buy in. Then, you can catch both the yard sales and the open houses and maybe find some vacant properties, too.

Vacant Houses

Vacant houses are a major source of houses that you can pick up for a song. Owners of these houses are usually motivated sellers. Nobody is making them offers. They aren't getting rent. When you come along and show some interest, what kind of reception do you think you are going to get? Most of the time, you'll be welcomed with open arms as a savior who can help them get something out of their problem house. Make them an offer, even a low-ball one, and they may just take it. If they pass it up, it will be a long time before anyone else comes along to buy it. Some of these house are ugly, decrepit heaps that nobody wants. Some of them are boarded up with condemned signs on them. You can pick them up real cheap. You'll get them so low that there will be plenty of room for repairs and plenty of profit for you and your buyer. I'll show you how you can find these houses and really make a killing.

They are not advertised, but they are all over the place if you look. Drive out to your target neighborhood. Ride around the neighborhood and look for vacant properties. If you find one in a neighborhood, you're likely to find several more in the area. Keep a little pocket recorder or PDA with you to record the address of all the vacant properties you see.

You may want to stop and ask the neighbors if they know who owns the property. Walk around the house and look for clues. There might be something lying around the house, maybe an old sign stuck out behind the house from an agent that listed the house at one time. Call the agent to get information on the name and address of the owner. Talk to the neighbors. Most of them know what is going on. Once you get back to the office, do an online search of the address to find the name of the property owner. There are many online search services to help find absentee owners. You can also use a skip tracer. Once you find the person, give them a call first. If you cannot get them on the phone, then send them a postcard or letter.

Finding Lost Homeowners   Here are a few services for tracking down homeowners: peoplesearch.net, www.searchsystems.net, www.white pages.com, www.nettrace.com.au, www.maralogix.com, www.merlindata .com, and www.findtheseller.com.

If you have tried these services and you still can't find the owner of a property, you may want to try this. Take a "For Sale By Owner" sign, put it in the yard with your number on it. Within a few days, the owner will call you to ask why you have a sign in her yard. I have never personally done this but one of my students told me about it, and it could work.

Here is another idea. Look up all of the owners on the street by searching the county web site. Then get their contact information from people finder web sites. Then call all of the neighbors to see what they know about the owner of the vacant property.

For Sale by Owner Signs   While you are riding around looking for vacant houses, you might see some "For Sale By Owner" signs. These owners are generally not as motivated as owners of vacant houses. Write down the address and telephone number, give them a call, and put them in your database. You will find a few properties this way. However, you will not find very many because it has been my experience that the people who are selling their houses themselves are too cheap to pay a realtor. So they are probably not going to take very much of a discount on their property unless it needs a lot of work. Don't worry about these too much because you are really looking for unadvertised properties. Let your autoresponder software do the work of following up with them.

Hire Others to Bring Vacant Houses to You   You should be making offers and closing deals. You shouldn't be driving around neighborhoods looking for vacant houses. Do it once or twice for the experience, then hire someone else to do this for you. Here's what I do to get hundreds of leads on vacant houses delivered to my door.

Find someone with a vehicle and a digital camera who has time to drive around neighborhoods looking for vacant houses. Pay them $5 for every vacant house they find and have them take a picture of each house. But before taking the picture have them put an erasable sign in the front of the house with the address written on it. You can get an erasable whiteboard from many office supply stores and use that to make a sign for each house. Take the picture. Then erase the sign and use it again for the next house.

When they bring you the pictures, pay them $5 for each picture. If they get the name and current address of the owner by asking around or looking it up on the computer give them another $10. It's worth every penny. I have one gal that does nothing but drive around neighborhoods bringing me leads. It's great. She makes good money in her spare time. And I close lots of deals worth $5,000 or more each!

Other Sources of Leads on Vacant Houses

Code Enforcement Agencies   There are many properties that are under code enforcement, which means that the property has code violations that do not meet minimum housing standards. If they cannot find the owner, sometimes they will publish a notice looking for the owner. Sometimes you can buy those properties pretty cheap if you can locate the owner. We have gotten some of the best deals through code enforcement.

Code enforcement agencies are one of my favorite ways to find vacant and run-down houses. Contact your local code enforcement agent and tell him or her what you do. Tell them if they send you leads, you will buy some of the houses they have on their books that are in violation of county codes and get them off their books.

Contact the agent in your county and in your surrounding counties. When you call the county, find out who the building inspector, minimum housing inspectors, or code enforcement officers are. Get their contact information: their phone, fax, and their e-mail. Some of them are online; some of them are not. Go and visit the ones that are online to find out if they have any properties with code violations on them. I have had some code enforcement officers welcome me into their offices, open the file drawer, pull open the files, and tell me about different properties that they can either not find the owner or cannot get the owner to fix up the property.

Don't be shy about asking for this information. This is public information. Some of the best deals that we have purchased have been through building inspectors. Once you buy one property that you got through the building inspector and sold to an investor who fixed it up, be sure to contact the inspector to let them know. Have them come out and look at it. Once your investor/buyer gets that property fixed up, the building inspector will be more open to looking for more deals for you in the future. They will start bringing deals to you.

Utility Workers   When someone leaves a house, they get their utilities shut off. That means a utility worker has to drive out to the house and shut off the water, power, or gas. Some of these houses having their utilities disconnected are properties that are available to buy. Any time you see a utility worker in a neighborhood, stop them and give them your card. Give them your big card that is 8-by-10 inches on corrugated plastic so they can put it in their vehicle to remember you when they see a vacant property.

Tell them you will give them $5 for every lead on a house that becomes vacant. Have them take a picture as described previously and give it to you. And offer them $10 if they give you the name and contact info of the owner. They can also scout out other vacant houses in the neighborhoods. You can do the same with garbage collection services, lawn care companies, and city bus drivers.

Homeowners in Transition   When people are in transition in their lives, they often need to sell real estate. But they are often not in a good financial position to take the time and expense to sell at full price. Here are sources for locating motivated homeowners in transition with houses to sell.

Attorneys   People in transition are often in contact with an attorney. Divorce is a major life change, and divorce attorneys are a good source of leads on houses for sale. Contact the attorney for the plaintiff, to see if there is any real estate involved. Let them know that you buy houses. Call them, fax them, e-mail them, and send them letters.

Another source is estate attorneys. When someone passes away, they usually have assets that need to be sold by the heirs. Contact estate attorneys who may be in touch with heirs who have inherited property that they want to dispose of.

Real estate attorneys know who is buying and selling and who has property for sale. Also look for trustees, bankruptcy trustees, and trustees for deeds of trust on houses that are in foreclosure. Network with attorneys, get on the inside and do business with them.

Once they know you and know what you can do for them, they will start calling you when they have clients with houses to sell quickly. You will have to have the attorney contact their client because they will not give out client contact information without the client's consent.

Executors of an Estate   Executors of an estate are usually relatives of someone who has passed away and are settling the estate. There may be real estate that has to be sold. You can find out information at your local courthouse and from attorneys as well.

Owners by Default

Bail Bonding Companies   Often, bail bonding companies take a deed to secure a bail bond. It happens that many bonding companies end up owning real estate just by default and may have some properties for sale. They end up with the property when someone skips bail. I know many bail bonding people who are in the real estate business, so this is a good source for property.

Surplus Property for Sale   Contact your city and ask for the city attorney to find out if they have any surplus property for sale. Sometimes, cities have surplus property, including real estate. This is a good way to find some deals. Although you will not find a lot of property, it is a source.

You can also contact your state's Department of Transportation (DOT) and ask the same thing. One of the best deals we have ever purchased was from the South Carolina DOT. It is a commercial property on a four-lane highway near the interstate. We purchased a portion through a realtor and the rest was surplus property purchased from the South Carolina DOT. I have a total of $52,000 in the property, and it is currently on the market for $350,000.

Nonprofits   Many times people donate their real property to charities and nonprofit organizations for a tax write-off when they do not have any use for it. However, the charities would rather have money than owning the property. So they are very eager to sell the property. I am actually looking at a property right now in Shelby, North Carolina. One day a man from a nonprofit organization called me up and said that someone had passed away and willed them a piece of property and they were going to sell it. He got my name from an attorney and wanted to know if I would be interested. I told him I was and made him an offer. I may eventually get the deal resulting in another $5,000 plus payday for me.

Mobile Home Dealers   Many mobile home dealers receive houses as trade-ins on mobile homes they sell. They are not in the business of selling houses. They don't want to fix them up and find a buyer. So you could do them a great service by taking these properties off their hands at a big discount in exchange for a quick cash close.

Defaults and Foreclosures

Besides the courthouse where you can find information on the most recent foreclosures and delinquent property taxes, there are also a number of other sources of defaults and foreclosures.

Process Servers   When someone has a foreclosure filed against them, process servers go out to deliver that notice of foreclosure.

Security Guards   Security guards in gated communities know when process servers are serving notices of foreclosure on a resident. I got this idea when one of the security guards in my development saw my SUV with my "I buy Houses" sign. One day he flagged me down and said, "Do you buy foreclosures?" "Yes, I do," I replied. He said, "Let me tell you about a property down the street that they came in to serve papers on." If you do not know any of the security guards, just introduce yourself and hand them your big business card to put on the wall so they will remember you.

Hard Money Lenders   I am a hard money lender. I have been very fortunate that we have only had to foreclose on a few properties. However, I am sure there are some hard money lenders out there who have had to foreclose on more. You may even want to run an ad in the paper, "I buy delinquent mortgages." Many of them will call. Hard money lenders do not want to have to foreclose on a property. And some of them don't know how and don't want to learn. They will appreciate a quick way to solve the problem of defaulted loans without foreclosure. Maybe you can contact the owner of the property and work something out with them.

Bankers, Mortgage Brokers, and Other Lenders   Many banks, savings and loans, and mortgage companies have a real estate owned (REO) department. Most of these departments are willing to sell these houses cheap just to get them off their books.

You may also find someone in the loss mitigation department who knows of people who are planning to refinance or who are behind on payments.

I have actually had lenders call me and give me information about people who are behind on their payments. They describe the property and ask me if I would be interested. They give me a little generic information about the property. They tell the borrower that they may have a solution for them and ask if they can give them my number.

It is a violation of Privacy Law for them to give you the borrower's personal information. Don't ask them. But after they talk to you and find out that you can do the deal, sometimes they will have the borrower call you. I have actually bought several properties this way.

Private Money Lenders   There are other private individuals out there with assets, such as an IRA, CDs, savings accounts, or checking accounts. They lend money to investors as short-term loans to purchase and rehab properties. Sometimes an investor might get behind on payments with them, and they need to sell the house fast instead of foreclosing.

Homeowner's Associations   Many condos and single-family residences have homeowner's associations. Sometimes people don't pay their associa-tion dues. The association puts out notices in the community newsletter, and sometimes, associations even go so far as to foreclose on the property.

Keep in mind that this is a junior lien if there is already a mortgage on the property. But it is a signal that the homeowner is in trouble and may need to sell quickly. You may want to contact the association and ask if they own any property and also ask about any delinquent dues or any properties in foreclosure.

Tired Landlords

Landlording can be a tough business. Many landlords are burnt out, fed up, and desperate for a way out. They might welcome your deal. Here are some easy ways to find them.

For Rent Signs   When you're out driving around, look for signs that say "for rent," "for sale," "rent to own," and "lease to own." Sometimes these are tired landlords, and they just want to get rid of the property. Call the owner and have a chat, you might find quite a few who are willing to negotiate with you. Also when you're online, search for "for rent," "for sale," "rent to own," and "lease to own" in ads. Copy and paste these terms into your property file to call and make an offer. If the property is "for sale" or "for lease," a lot of times that means they may even owner finance that property.

Eviction Courts   Another place to find tired landlords is just outside of eviction court. Many landlords are already disgusted, and you may catch them when they are ready to sell just after having to evict the tenant. Simply find out what day your county holds eviction court and go there and wait for the landlords to come out. When they come out, hand them your "I Buy Houses" card, and ask if they have any property they may be interested in selling.

Damaged Houses

Insurance Companies   Insurance companies and insurance adjusters are a good place to find houses with damage. They know the properties that are in need of repair, and they know the properties that have claims. I have purchased properties from insurance companies that have paid a claim on the fire damage of a house.

Fire Departments   Fire departments keep records of all house fires. They know where the houses are with fire damage. They may be able to help you out as well by letting you know any time there is another property with fire damage.

Farming a Market

You can go right into the neighborhoods and go canvassing house to house looking for houses with motivated sellers to buy. Realtors do this all the time and call it farming the market. Canvassing is simply walking the neighborhoods, ringing doorbells, and reading a script at the door to the homeowner. If nobody is home or doesn't answer, then you put door hangers on the doors.

You could target people who you know are in preforeclosure or just go up to everyone in neighborhoods where you want to buy houses. You want to be careful when canvassing, especially if you are female and/or you are hiring others to do it for you. You never know who will answer the door.

Now you've got buyers, and you've got sellers. But there is one more thing you need before you start making offers and closing deals. You need money. The next chapter tells you how to get it.

CHAPTER 7
SECRETS OF DAY FUNDING: GET 24-HOUR FAST CASH

Someone very wise in the ways of the world once said, "He who has the cash, makes the rules." It's true. When you have money, you have power. People pay attention.

You can close deals with no money at all. And in this chapter, I explain how you can use options, flex options, assignments, simultaneous closings, and other techniques to close your day trade deals without any money. These techniques don't work for every deal. They don't even work for half the deals. Most of the time when we buy a house, we close the deal with cash. Then we turn around the same day and sell the house for cash. We buy and sell for cash in the same day.

For example, we agree to buy a house from our motivated seller for $50,000. After we do our due diligence, we announce the house for sale to our buyers for $60,000. We set a closing date. Then at closing, we show up with a check for $50,000, which we "borrowed" from our checking account. When we buy the house in the morning, we give the closing agent the check for $50,000. In the afternoon, the buyer shows up with a check for $60,000, which the closing agent gives us, and we deposit it into our account. We've returned the $50,000 we "borrowed" from our account that morning, plus a $10,000 profit. Now this example obviously doesn't include closing costs, but I left those out to keep things simple for this example.

That's how a typical day trade works. As you can see, we really didn't invest the money in real estate. We just funded the deal for a few hours between the closing in the morning when we bought the house and the closing that afternoon when we sold the house. Now in the real world, we would probably not receive the check from the seller until the next day because all of the documents would need to be recorded before the attorney or title company could disperse the funds, but you get the idea.

SHOW ME THE MONEY

Sometimes we get a contract from the seller, and when we close, we assign the contract to the buyer and receive a fee. And sometimes we can do a simultaneous closing, where we use the buyer's cash to pay the seller. But what about all the great opportunities we negotiate to buy bank-owned houses at rock-bottom prices from bank REO departments?

REO departments will refuse to work with you unless you have cash. They don't allow assignments or accept options. They know you are a serious buyer when you show up with cash. If not, you're just another looky-loo who's trying to waste their time. Once you get some cash in your pocket, you can snatch up preforeclosures, bank REOs, and houses at auction. Remember, you'll need cash to close any deal that you do through a realtor.

The more offers you can make, the more $5,000 plus paydays you'll have. Think of all the profitable deals you'll have to pass up if you don't have cash. With money, you'll be able to act decisively when a good deal comes along because you know you can pull out your checkbook and write a check for the property on the spot. Sellers can sense this and will be more willing to accept your low-ball offer because they know you are going to follow through.

That said, where do you get the cash?

WHERE YOU DON'T GET THE MONEY

First I want to tell you where not to get the money. As I mentioned previously, we're looking for overnight cash that will be out of pocket for 24 hours. We only need enough to buy a house for cash and then turn around and sell it for cash the same day. The money can then be returned to your bank account that day or the next.

We don't need to go to the bank and get a mortgage. Banks are out of the question anyway because they don't lend money on houses that are in need of repair. They won't lend based on after-repair appraised value. They will typically only lend up to 80 percent of the purchase price. They are only interested in lending to investors or owner occupants of fully repaired houses. When your investors/buyers sell the house at retail, banks finance the purchase for the new homeowner.

We don't need to get a loan from hard money lenders, private money, partners, or investors. These are the kinds of lenders that your investors/buyers will use to buy the house from you and to rehab and sell or lease it. For example, private lenders want to lend money at a fixed rate for a fixed term—usually about 12 to 15 percent for a year. Private lending will not work for you because your private money lender wants to sit back and collect interest for 6 to 12 months. But you only want the money for 24 hours to close the deal. They won't earn much interest lending money for just one day.

And hard money lenders usually charge 4 to 7 points, plus 12 to 15 percent for a maximum of one year. It would be very expensive to use a hard money lender for just a day. You'd pay 6 points upfront just to get the funds released to you plus all of their fees. Getting money from partners is just as expensive unless it is your only source.

Where, then, does this leave us? How do we find the short-term, 24-hour money we need to lock in these deals? It is not really a problem. If you have a good deal, the money will come. You'll find many sources of cash if you start looking. Just think of it this way. You don't need a lot of money, just enough to close the deal—around $50,000 per deal or maybe more on more expensive houses. Now remember, even though you may live in an area where the prices are much more, by day trading the way I have taught you, you can buy properties anywhere and in any market. But as I've explained, the majority of the houses we buy are going to be cheap. Second, we only need the money for one day at a time. Then we return the money to the lender.

Your lender can sleep like a baby knowing the money they lent in the morning is back in their coffers in 24 hours. They don't have to be concerned that you are spending the money recklessly, that cost overrides are going to wipe you out, or that some emergency will cost you more cash. All they know is that you paid them back the same day. That makes a good impression.

You'll find plenty of lenders who will want to deal with you. First let me explain how you can access some of the cheapest money on the planet. And it will cost you nothing to use.

BORROW ON YOUR CREDIT CARDS

Credit cards are a good source of funds if you use them correctly. If you're like me, you've got a wallet full of credit cards, with $5,000 to $10,000 lines of credit on every one of them. Most credit cards come with checks, so using your credit card is as simple as writing a check. Maybe right now, you don't have enough credit cards or high enough credit limits to fund a closing with them. But you can apply for more cards and get credit limit increases on the others to build your available cash.

One of my students has $250,000 in available credit on his credit cards. Now whenever he needs cash for a day trade he writes a check. He doesn't have to fill out an application or qualify. As a card member, all he has to do is use the funds that the bank has made available to him.

To raise the credit limit on the card, just call the credit card company and request a credit limit increase. If they ask why, tell them you are expecting to spend more using the card. Telling them you are going to use it for business expenses. If you have a $5,000 credit limit, ask them to raise it to $10,000. If you have a $10,000 credit limit, then ask for a $25,000 credit limit. They might give it to you right away, or they might check your credit. Keep your credit good, and you won't have any problem. Only do this on two to three cards a month because too many inquiries on your credit report will lower your score.

Also, apply for some of the credit card offers that come in the mail or search the Internet for the best deals. Some come with no annual fee, long grace periods, and low interest. I like to use the rewards cards best because I get frequent flyer miles. That's very important given the high cost of air travel these days. Many cards offer 5 percent cash back and no-interest introductory offers. Creditratings.com has a wide selection of credit cards to choose from, MasterCard, Visa, Discover, and the Blue Card from American Express. American Express offers a credit card called American Express OPEN with no credit limit for business owners. You just have to establish a track record of using the card in successively higher amounts and over time, you will be authorized to charge $30,000 to $50,000 or more for business use.

If you don't have good credit, you can find a friend or relative with good credit who knows and trusts you to apply for the credit cards for your use. Always pay them back the same day or within 24 hours.

BORROW ON YOUR LIFE INSURANCE

If you own a life insurance policy that you've been paying on for a number of years, you can get a loan within days up to 100 percent of the cash surrender value. And the rates are very low. Just be sure to pay it back and never put it at risk.

BORROW ON YOUR HOME

If you have equity in your home, arrange for a second mortgage. Lenders will usually loan up to 70 percent to 80 percent of the appraised value of the home. If you currently owe $120,000 on a house appraised at $200,000, you can refinance and get a second mortgage of up to 80 percent of the appraised value or $160,000. This leaves $40,000 (less points and closing costs), which you can put into your day trading fund.

OPEN RESERVE CHECKING ACCOUNTS

Many banks offer reserve checking accounts, meaning that you will have a reserve in your checking account that allows you to write checks for more than the amount you have in the account. It is also known as an overdraft protection account. Some banks will require that you have a regular account in good standing before they'll accept you for the cash reserve account. Certain banks only require that the interest be paid on a monthly basis. Other banks require a percentage of the balance be paid monthly as well.

It's not uncommon for banks to give a credit limit of $5,000 to $10,000 to its customers. Open bank accounts at banks and credit unions that offer this service. Before opening the account, make sure they offer overdraft protection first. If you are approved for $5,000 in overdraft protection at 10 banks, you'll have $50,000 within your grasp. Don't spend a penny of it on anything but funding your deals. Pay the money back promptly after closing the deal.

BORROW FROM YOUR SELF-DIRECTED IRA

Yes, you can use your IRA to fund your deals, but there are some restrictions on this. First, you have to have a self-directed IRA from a custodian like Equity Trust. I have had an account with them for years. They are great to work with and very well-known among real estate investors. Once you set up an account and either transfer an existing IRA to them or fund a new one, you can then start using the money in the IRA to buy properties.

Remember that when buying real estate with your self-directed IRA, you cannot have a mortgage on it unless it is a nonrecourse loan. These are very difficult to get so here is how we use our IRA to buy property.

You can use it when day trading a property that requires all cash. You simply write on the contract "Equity Trust for the Benefit of, Your Name" as the buyer. In fact, the custodian will show you what to do. Then your IRA will send the funds to the seller's attorney, title company, or closing agent. And when you sell the house the same day to another investor and collect your fee, it goes right back into your IRA. If you have a traditional IRA, this transaction will be tax deferred, and if you have a Roth IRA, it will be totally tax free. You can use it when buying with an option if you only have a small amount of money in your IRA.

Here is another way to buy using your IRA. If you are buying a property you can assign, you can buy it in the name of your IRA and then assign the contract to another investor. The money you used for a deposit comes from the IRA, and the money you make when you assign it goes back into your IRA as well. This is a great way to take a small amount of money and build it to a large IRA account.

Another good idea that I have used as well is to find another investor who also has a self-directed IRA and loan each other money at a good rate of return; then, it's like getting the same rate of return on your IRA or borrowing the money for *free*.

Here is another idea for growing your IRA quickly. As you start buying and selling more and more houses, I would suggest that for every five to ten houses you day trade, you buy one in your IRA. This is very easy to do, and because you are already buying property anyway, you just switch the name of the buyer from your company name to your IRA.

Here's a way you could fund your kid's college and prepare for retirement as well. Once you get going in your day trading business, you could open up an education IRA for your kids, a SIMPLE IRA for your business, and even the new personal 401(k). If your children are old enough, you could actually put them on the payroll and fund an IRA for them. See your CPA for more information on this.

Warning, don't go to your brokerage firm and try to get them to do this. They'll tell you that it's impossible. They will carefully explain that they know everything about self-directed IRA's because they handle them for many of their clients. And they'll say they've never heard of anyone ever using a self-directed IRA to buy real estate. They might even claim it's illegal. Don't listen to them.

What they don't tell you is that they have carefully designed their IRAs to include only the investments, mutual funds, stocks, bonds, CDs, and money market funds they offer. What they offer are not true self-directed IRAs. The rules governing self-directed IRAs are much broader than they would lead you to believe. Have your self-directed IRA transferred to a custodian who knows and understands buying and selling real estate through a self-directed IRA. I've had great success using Equity Trust for doing real estate transactions through my IRA. You can find out more at their web site www.TrustETC.com.

SELL NONESSENTIAL, PERSONAL POSSESSIONS ON EBAY

Do you own a second car, truck, boat, motorcycle, mobile home, or summer home? Raise cash by selling it through the classifieds, or on eBay. Tap into all your accumulated possessions that are nonessential: an extra TV, computer, music system, sports equipment, fishing gear, golf clubs, camping, hunting gear, books, CDs, furniture, and jewelry. Put it all up for sale if you're not using it. Add all the proceeds into your fund. You can replace these items with new ones once you start day trading two to three properties a month and earning multiple $5,000 plus paydays.

Selling things on eBay is easy and fast. And you get much more money than you would if you tried to sell to pawnshops, at flee markets, in classified ads, or in yard sales. My wife sells literally anything on eBay, and she only works a few hours a week. She makes more money than she did when she was a schoolteacher. She started out selling things around the house we no longer were using.

Now she goes to yard sales and buys things to resell on eBay at a profit. Be sure to put all the proceeds into a special account for saving money to fund your deals. Keep at it, and it won't be long until you are just a few sales away from having enough money to make deposits and day trade houses. Soon, you'll have the cash to do assignment and option deals.

USE UNSECURED PEER-TO-PEER LENDING SITES

Peer-to-peer lending is people who want to borrow money, seeking people who want to lend money to them. To be listed as a borrower, you typically need at least a 640 credit score, plus income and expense documentation. You can borrow up to $25,000 on each loan you make.

Lenders on these sites decide whether or not to lend to a particular individual, based on the borrower's credit score and amount of current debt. But these sites are different from banks because the decision is based on personal factors that bankers usually don't consider. For example, if you have a compelling reason for requesting the loan, it could carry weight with some lenders. Also sharing a hobby in common will sway certain lenders to take a chance on lending to you. You get a chance to tell your story and get people to understand your situation.

Once you explain what you do and that you are not only not going to spend the money, but instead, return it to your checking account the same day, many lenders will be impressed and feel secure lending to you. These loans are reported to the credit bureaus and will show up on your credit report. Usually you get lower rates than credit cards because lenders compete with each other to make a loan to you. This results in lower rates than credit cards, typically in the 10 to 15 percent range. But in day trading, the cost of funds is not the issue, the availability of funds is much more important. And peer-to-peer sites offer you a ready source of fast cash.

There are two types of peer-to-peer lending sites:

1. Pooled lending is when the lender lends the money to a pool of borrowers with similar credit ratings. Zopa.com and LendingClub.com are examples of pooled lending clubs. Lending Club is open to U.S. residents. To qualify for funding, you need a FICO score of at least 640 and a debt-to-income ratio (excluding mortgage) below 30 percent. They also require that you have no current delinquencies and at least 12 months of credit history.

2. Direct lending is when the lender lends you money based on your credit rating. Visit Kiva.com, VirginMoneyUS.com, and Prosper.com for examples of direct lenders.

GET SMALL BUSINESS LOANS ONLINE

Fund your deals with a small business loan. There are many companies that offer small business loans online in minutes. For example, Unsecured Solutions.com offers unsecured loans from $10,000 to $100,000, and no documents are required. AmOne.com makes $50,000 small business loans with no collateral required. Access-Capital-Funding.com will lend you up to $50,000 even if you have bad credit. Ezunsecured.com provides unsecured business lines up to $350,000 with no income documentation and up to $1,000,000 with full documentation. And CapNetUSA.com offers working capital loans from $1,000 to $150,000. Be sure to add these web sites to your bookmarks under the category of Real Estate Funding.

TRY SHORT-TERM BUSINESS LOANS

Business loans are much easier to get than personal loans, and they are obtainable even if your credit is weak. In addition, interest rates are lower, the bank requires you to pay off the loan less frequently, the loans are easier to renew, and business loans receive more favored treatment at the bank. The reason is that business loans are generally less risky than personal loans.

When someone borrows money for personal reasons, he or she usually spends the money. The money is gone and must be repaid from personal income. Business loans are much different. The proceeds are invested in the business to produce income and make a profit. The income is then used to repay the loan with interest.

Short-term business loans are the easiest and fastest to get. The bigger the amount and the longer the term, the more cautious the bank becomes. They want to be your lender, not your partner. For this reason you will find it much easier to obtain a short-term loan for your business. You must have a business, a corporation, LLC, or S-Corp. These are easy to form. There are numerous web sites that can help you incorporate a business or form an LLC in 48 hours for under $200. Open an account at a commercial bank and deposit all the funds you have been accumulating.

There are many, and you can find them by performing a Google search of "unsecured business credit."

USE MICROLENDERS

Microlending organizations are a great source for very small companies that have been turned down by banks. Many commercial banks will not make commercial loans under $50,000. Generally, they are unwilling to take the risk of investing in very small start-up businesses and avoid loans that are not fully secured by collateral.

Microlending was created to fill this gap. A microloan is $25,000 or less made to a company with five or fewer employees. The industry average microloan is $12,000. There are 600 to 700 microlenders currently in operation in the United States. Most get their funding from federal, state, and local grants; along with donations from private philanthropy, including religious, minority, and women's groups.

For example, Count Me In is an online microcreditor that offers small business financing from $5,000 to $50,000 for women-owned startup businesses. ACCION United States and its partners have lent over $154 million to more than 16,000 women and men across the country. It is the largest microlending network in the United States, with offices in San Diego, Miami, Atlanta, Chicago, Boston, Albuquerque, New York, and San Antonio.

FIND DAY FUNDERS

Instead of looking for private lenders, look for what I call *day funders*. In day funding you only need a small amount of money, about $50,000, to complete most of your day trades for all cash in 24 hours.

You could offer your day funder an overnight interest rate of 1 percent. On $50,000, that would be $500 that is fully backed by the title of the property until paid in full the same day. What could be easier and more profitable for an investor? I can tell you there are many private investors who would love to day fund this deal.

Private investors usually lend money at 12 percent per year. If they lend $50,000, they would make $500 in interest a month. But you are offering them $500 to borrow $50,000 for 24 hours. And you are going to do three to four deals a month.

And there's much less risk. Day funders have complete control of their money 29 days out of the month. At the end of the day, the money is safely back in the day funder's account earning interest. The day funders funds held in escrow are refundable if the deal doesn't close. The investor has peace of mind knowing that his or her money is always under the control of the closing agent.

You can easily cover the cost of this day funder fee by accounting for the $500 cost of funding in your instant property analysis, and thereby lowering your maximum allowable bid on the property by $500. So after closing you'll collect $5,500 and give $500 to the lender, keeping $5,000 for yourself.

If you can't find day funders to make you 24-hour loans for $500, then you could offer them $1,000, $2000, or even half of your profit if you have to in order to get the deal closed. Just remember, I would rather have a little of something than all of nothing.

There are many people with money who would like to lend it out at an excellent rate of return. They basically fall into two classes, the sophisticated investor and the unsophisticated saver.

I call the sophisticated investors, *angels*. They have a long track record of investing in small start-up companies and commercial and residential real estate. Some specialize in single-family houses. They usually participate as private lenders. The kind of deal you are offering them is very appealing. You won't have to explain or convince them to get into the deal. They'll either do it or they won't. It depends mostly on the kinds of deals they want to do.

Savers are a different brand altogether. They are used to savings accounts, certificates of deposit (CDs), mutual funds, money market funds, and the like. Most have 401(k)s and IRAs and are used to the investments being pushed on them by banks and brokerages. If they are new to real estate, it may take a little more explaining and hand-holding to deal with them.

How do you find money? A lot of people suggest having seminars and luncheons to find money. I do not think you need to do this to find a day funder. It's too complicated and time consuming. You have to get your priorities straight. Are you looking for houses or are you looking for money? You really want to be looking for houses. So you want to go the fastest, cheapest, quickest way to get the funds to close your deal, so that you can concentrate on buying property to get your machine up and running.

And it's unnecessary if you are seeking a reliable source of day funding. Finding and dealing with "angels" is the easiest and fastest way to get your day funding. Most angels operate through business associates and friends and invest close to where they live. The easiest way and least costly way to find a lender is to network.

Start publicizing your day funding deals at your local Real Estate Investors Association events. Go in and find out who the players are, who is buying and selling property, and ask all of them to tell you about the individuals with money to lend. Make a flyer describing your deal and give it to everyone who's interested.

The neat thing about dealing with angels is that you do not have to be concerned about being self-employed, what your debt ratio is, your credit or your experience, because the investor is basically investing their money in the property itself with you standing behind the deal.

Because angels tend to congregate in the same social and business circles, once you have two or three individuals day funding your deals and getting a good return on their funds, these angel investors will tell their friends. It won't be long before you have other angels contact you about loaning out their money to you for a day at a time, at a good rate of return.

In order to attract private money in the beginning, you are going to need a credibility kit or at least some information on who you are, what you have done, where you have bought and sold property. Especially show how much the day funder made on each deal. If you have not done that, you need to team up with somebody and get a couple of deals under your belt so you can build your credibility kit pretty quickly. You want to be able to prove to them that you can keep their money safe while earning a good rate of return.

If you don't find a day funder in your local real estate group, then you should network to other business groups. In your local area there are hundreds of people with money to lend who are always on the lookout for a good opportunity. They don't all belong to your real estate association.

Networking in your community has two stages. The first stage is to attend events sponsored by various business groups, the Chamber of Commerce, Rotary Club, Kiwanis, Optimist Club, Jaycees, and so on. Investment clubs are also good places to meet potential lenders. Be sure to attend the events that allow you to mix and mingle with the other guests so that you can make new contacts and avoid events that feature speakers but do not allow you to meet people and expand your network. You can also use this opportunity to network for buyers and sellers to add to your database.

Pay special attention to the events put on by the many entrepreneur groups that are springing up all across the country. These kinds of groups are usually very keen on networking, and many of the guests are suppliers of capital. Your goal in attending these events is strictly business. You're attending for the purpose of making contact with individuals who can lend money to your company or who know someone who can lend money to fund your deals. People like bankers, attorneys, accountants, management consultants, financial planners, realtors, and insurance brokers are very good contacts because they often know when one of their clients is looking for a place to invest some money. Once you've broken the ice at a business mixer, it won't be hard to get appointments to present your deal to some viable prospects.

Also, do some nonbusiness related networking. Churches and clubs are also a great place to look for lenders. Going to the same church, belonging to the same club, or living in the same neighborhood gives you something in common. Many of the people you see every day have some cash or a portfolio that they would like to get a better rate of return on.

One of the best and quickest ways I know of to get funding is this. Every time you meet someone new or see someone (even at the gas pumps or in the store or elevator, etc.) ask them what they do for a living. After they reply (e.g., "I'm an engineer"), they will always ask you what you do for a living. That's your cue to say, "I help engineers become wealthy investing in real estate." Then this opens the door for you to tell them about what you do and how they can invest passively with you and earn a good rate of return. I learned this technique from my good friend and life coach Raymond Aaron.

A lot of people like to invest their own IRA money. If they are willing to get a self-directed IRA at a company like Equity Trust, they can invest their money with you, loaning it out for a day at a time, and get a fabulous rate of return, much greater than the amount they are getting with the stock market or mutual funds.

Get the Names and Addresses of Angel Investors in Your Area

One of the most successful ways to find private lenders fast, and not a lot of people will tell you this, is to ask around your real estate club and find the names of investors who are using private lenders.

Once you find out the names of other investors who use private money for their deals, then all you have to do is search the courthouse records and find out who the private lenders are on their deals. Then you can contact them to see if they would like to also become one of your day funders.

Consider Partners Carefully

Real estate day funders are not partners. Silent partners usually get 50 percent of the profits for putting up 100 percent of the money. In day funding, you don't need long-term money. And you don't need partners. They take too much of the profits for what they offer. All you need is money for 24 hours to close the deal. You don't need a partner involved in your business. If you are going to have a partner make sure that each partner has something unique to contribute to the partnership.

If you would like to have me fund your day funding deal, I would be glad to. In fact, I can even give you a proof of funds letter to give to your seller or realtor showing that you have the funds to close. All I need is your seller's information, your buyer's information, the property information, and the closing attorney or title company to wire the money to. You do not even need good credit or have to fill out an application. Just go to www.realestatedaytrading.com and click on the link for day funding.

CHAPTER 8

ASSEMBLE YOUR VIRTUAL
ONLINE DREAM TEAM

Day trading houses depends on pin-
point timing. Once your motivated sellers sign a contract with you to sell
their house for cash, you need to move fast. As mentioned previously, you
must have a database of motivated buyers and the financing to do an all-cash
close.

But before you announce it to your buyers list, send a rehab contractor to
inspect the house and give you an accurate repair estimate. Then give your
appraiser the inspection report and ask him to report the after-repair value.
When you announce the property, you can provide your investors/buyers
with an accurate estimate of repair and appraisal. This will make it easy for
your buyers to give you a contract right away without a lot of deliberation.
Doing everything quickly and efficiently is the key to success in real estate
day trading.

To close this deal fast and make your payday, you also need an experienced
real estate attorney or title and escrow service, an appraiser, and a home
inspection service. They all play a pivotal role in getting deals done rapidly.
Don't leave these things for the last minute. You want to prescreen these
professionals in advance to make sure they are willing and able to play a key
role in your dream team.

WITH REAL ESTATE CONTRACTORS,
PROFESSIONALISM IS EVERYTHING

You're going to day trade the house; you're not going to rehab it. So why
do you need a rehab contractor? It's simple. You want your investor/buyer

to buy your house sight unseen in one day. You've got to give your buyers the solid proof they need to make this decision.

You've got to set yourself apart from the crowd by showing that you are acting in the best interest of the buyer. Having a reputable rehab contactor go in and inspect the house and come back with a realistic bid on repairing it shows that you are operating at a higher standard. You don't want the contractor for yourself; you want the contractor for your buyer. You want the bid to be honest and accurate. That's what will help you sell houses fast.

The kind of contactor you want depends on the size of the job. When we talk about rehabbing houses, we are talking about work that will cost between $5,000 and $20,000, sometimes more. We're not talking about a small maintenance or repair job that will take a couple of hours. If your house just needs a few hours of work, then all you need is a handyman.

Depending on who your buyer is, they may or may not use the rehab contractor who inspects the job and submits a bid. Many investors/buyers are contractors or handymen and will do the work themselves. Some will act as general contractors on the job and hire and manage their subcontractors to save money. They'll get separate bids for carpentry, electrical work, plumbing, carpeting, flooring, drywall and plastering, roofing, masonry, and HVAC. But for your purposes, to give them an accurate estimate of the cost of the entire rehab job, you want to use a general contractor.

Know What You Are Looking For

After they buy the house from you, your buyers might want to hire sub-contractors and manage them. That's okay. But right now you are looking for a licensed general contractor who is ready, willing, and able to give you a reliable bid. Even though you are not going to use this contractor yourself, you want the person to be able to do the job in a reasonable time at a reasonable price. The prices charged by licensed general contractors are higher than the prices charged by unlicensed contractors. But it is well worth the extra cost to get bids from licensed contractors.

For one thing, a general contractor takes full responsibility for the entire project. They are your investor's manager in charge and hire and manage all the subs. They make sure the subcontractors show up and do the work they are getting paid for. Consider it a management fee. If your investors/buyers later decide to forego paying this fee in exchange for their own time and effort, that's their decision. But the cost of managing should be included as part of the repair cost.

Find Good Rehab Contractors

Some ways to locate good rehab contracts include:

- *Yellow Pages:* The first place many people look is the Yellow Pages. You will find a lot of residential general contractors here. But most of them are retail contractors targeting homeowners. It won't hurt to call them and find out if they do rehabs for investors. And if not, then ask them if they know of a licensed general contractor who does.
- *Community newspapers:* Many residential general contractors advertise their services in local and neighborhood newspapers. Look in the classified ads under "Services" in newspapers that cover the neighborhoods where you are buying houses. Many contractors like to get jobs close to where they live.
- *Online searches:* Start your online search going to Google and entering the keywords "general contractor your city." You can also search the online directories of Yahoo.com, Google.com, and Dmoz.org. If you want to get a lot of listings quickly, search the online yellow pages such as BrightPages.com, SuperPages.com, and Yellowbook.com.

  You can also use online services that allow you to post your rehab project free and get bids from local contractors: BidClerk .com, Remodelers-Online.com, ReliableRemodeler.com, Service Magic.com, Contractors.Respond.com, RenovationExperts.com, and BuildingPros.com. But be careful because many of them are retail contractors targeting homeowners. Maybe they will give you wholesale pricing if you promise them repeat business.
- *Networking:* Network with your online and offline investor groups. Distribute flyers at your local real estate association and make an announcement on the real estate forums and your social networking sites. Print an "I Hire General Contractors" flyer to use when networking at groups.

  Many investors and contractors are in these groups. Many of them do rehabs for investors or know somebody who does rehabs for investors. You should also attend contractor and building construction trade groups. To find the ones in your local area, search online using the keywords, "residential contractors association your city," "residential builders association your city," "building contractors association your city," and "construction trade groups your city."

  Use your database of realtors to get general contractor referrals. In Chapter 6, I told you how to find the best realtors for bank-owned property. Just ask a realtor friend to give you a list of the properties that have already sold with the keywords "REO," "Bank-Owned," "Seller Addendum required," and "Foreclosure." These are the agents you want to deal with. Add them to your database and put them into your autoresponder series for realtors. As a part of this series, many of the e-mail follow-up messages you create should ask them for referrals to well-qualified contractors with good reputations.

Many realtors will reply with the name of a good contractor. If the same name keeps coming up, you'll know you have your contractor. You can do the same with your autoresponder messages to the investors/buyers on your database.

- *Prospecting:* Start prospecting at contractor supply stores. The obvious ones are Home Depot and Lowes. But you could also target the outlets that cater to builders on a wholesale level. Search online with the keywords, "contractors supply your city," "building materials your city," and "construction equipment rental your city." Drive to these places early in the morning and try to get there right after they open. Ask around about licensed general contractors who do rehab work on houses. Distribute your "I Hire General Contractors" flyers. Look for business cards near the checkout or on the bulletin boards. Ask the clerk if he or she knows a licensed contractor who does rehab work on houses.

  Approach some of the contractors who are there. Talk to them and get their business cards. If they don't have a business card, it's probably a good sign they aren't professional enough for you. Check out their vehicles. If they have a sign advertising their company on their truck, it's a good sign they are running a reputable business.

  As a word of warning, don't bother to use the rehab departments of Home Depot or Lowes. They don't really offer a general contracting service. They will usually send out subs to give you bids on parts of the job, not a general contractor to oversee the entire job. And, most of the bids you'll get from big chains are overpriced.

  Also, drive around the neighborhoods where your houses are located and look for rehabbers on the job. Talk to them and get their business cards. Then look at the work they are doing. Notice the details. Are they slow and unfocused? Is the work sloppy? Is the whole area disorderly? You can tell a lot about people by the way they work.

- *Searching city records:* If you want to find licensed general contractors, go down to city hall or wherever the city records are kept; look up the licensed building contractors and make a list of their names, addresses, phone numbers, and license numbers. Take this list and input it in your database of contractors.

Then follow up with an autoresponder series that introduces your firm to them, tells them you are looking to give them repeat business, and asks them if they would like to be notified when you have a house in need of repairs for them to inspect and bid on. By contacting them you will find out which ones are good and willing to do business on your terms.

Prescreen General Rehab Contractors

You want to make sure your repair bids are coming from people who are honest, reputable, and professional. There are lots of good contractors out there. You just have to find them. Here are some ways to separate the wheat from the chaff.

First, make sure the contractor is licensed. You want licensed contractors only. Why? Because to become a licensed general contractor, a person has to invest money in getting a license and get enough education to pass a test that shows they understand the state's building codes and the procedures for getting permits. This weeds out the flaky part-timers who will waste your time and your money. This will enable you to check out contractors you meet online and through networking and prospecting who tell you they are licensed. You can check the list to see if they are on it, if their license has expired, or if they are using the license number of a friend or someone they work for.

You also want to make sure they are bonded and insured. It's risky letting someone without insurance work on your property. If there is an accident, you could be sued. Ask them to show you their current certificates. Make sure the contractor has adequate liability coverage.

Also ask for references. Most investors ask for three references and end up with three relatives who will vouch for this contractor no matter what he does. I always ask for five references. In addition to the three most people ask for, I ask for two others.

I ask for the material supplier where the contractor buys supplies. If the contractor doesn't have an account with a supplier, that's a bad sign. If he or she does, I always check with the supplier to find out how long the contractor has been buying from that supplier. Once, a contractor told me three years and the supply store told me three weeks. That's a big difference.

Be sure to call the Better Business Bureau to find out if there are any serious complaints concerning the contractor. Also check on AngiesList .com—a word-of-mouth network for people to report their firsthand experiences with general contractors. It is organized by area. Members from your area tell you who to use and who to avoid.

Here are warning flags that a contractor is bad and should be avoided: *no phone number listed, offers special prices if you act fast, gives you a low-ball offer, works with substandard materials, asks you to pull permits, and wants to be paid all cash in advance.*

Remember, you want somebody who has invested in the career of contracting and has made a financial and educational commitment to being a professional. If you take the time to prescreen contractors as I've explained, you will have some reliable professional contractors to inspect your houses and give you accurate repair estimates.

You need to establish up front that you are an investor and that their bids must be accurate and affordable. They won't get away with overcharging. And you want fast turnaround on the inspections—no more than two days. In exchange, you promise them repeat business. You buy dozens of houses a year. And you resell these houses to buyers/investors who will fix them up for retailing or renting. You will be a source of a lot of business for them.

FOR APPRAISERS, AVAILABILITY IS THE KEY

Many appraisers have more work than they can handle. Most are understaffed and are very busy keeping up with the demands of their clients. They work for the clients who bring them the most business and bother them the least. They hate working with homeowners who tend to be too emotionally attached to the outcome of the appraisal and who need too much hand-holding. They like to deal with mortgage brokers and loan officers who are more professional and know what they are doing.

When talking to appraisers, make sure you make it clear that you buy a lot of houses, and you can send them a lot of appraisals, and that you will pay in advance. That will get their attention. They don't like waiting for money or chasing past-due balances.

In exchange, tell them what you require. You want availability. You want them to be able to drop what they are doing and do your appraisal in no more than two days. The houses you typically deal in—bread-and-butter houses—are not difficult or complicated; they are just simple three-bedroom, two-bath houses. They should have no trouble doing your appraisals fast. Being able to get fast, accurate appraisals is important and the key to your success.

You also want to work with one that will give you a good conservative appraisal and will not push the values just to make a deal work. Make sure your appraiser understands this.

Find a Good Appraiser

In my experience, appraisers are easy to find and easy to work with if you can show them what's in it for them. Don't come across as an amateur or needy homeowner. Approach appraisers in a businesslike way. Show them a win-win situation, and they will work with you. Places to find good appraisers include:

- *Yellow Pages:* Many appraisers in your area will be listed in the Yellow Pages. But not all of them are listed. Many of the ones who deal mostly with mortgage companies don't bother to advertise themselves. They don't need to.
- *Online searches:* You can build your database of appraisers quickly by doing a few online searches. Search "real estate appraisers your city" or "real estate appraisals your city." Also try searching these directories: GoodRealEstateAppraiser.com, HomeCheck.com, Alamode .com, and NeedAppraisers.com.
- *Networking:* Again, you should network with your online and offline investor groups. Search your social networking groups for other members who are involved in real estate and residential appraisals. Also ask the realtors you are working with for a referral.

Prescreen Appraisers

Make sure every property appraiser you work with is licensed or certified by the state to perform real estate appraisals. This shows that the appraiser has met the minimum standards required by the state to do real estate appraisals. This is important. Ask the appraiser if they can do what is called a *subject to* appraisal, sometimes known as an *as repaired* appraisal. This means that they will estimate the value of the property after the repairs are complete. You will give the appraiser the repair estimate and tell them to appraise the property as if the repairs were complete.

Also ask the appraiser if he or she has a professional designation. The standards for getting these special designations are often greater than the requirements for being licensed. The most common professional appellations for appraisers are Member, American Institute of Real Estate Appraisers (MAI); Senior Residential Appraiser (SRA); or Senior Real Property Appraiser (SRPA). These designations show that the appraiser is committed to continuing professional education and maintaining high ethical standards.

Ask appraisers if they have done appraisals in the parts of town where you are buying houses. Favor the appraisers who do a lot of work in or live in the areas where you are buying houses. By working in an area, the appraiser learns about the neighborhoods, school districts, fire departments, developments, and zoning that may have an effect on the property value of your house.

WHEN CHOOSING A TITLE COMPANY, SERVICE IS KING

In some states, you will use a title company, and in others, you will use an attorney to close your transaction. Any realtor can tell you which one to use.

Title companies play an important role. They make sure that the real estate transactions are handled efficiently and accurately. Once you sign a contract, you have the right to request any title company you want to handle your closing. The title company holds earnest money in an escrow account until the final settlement and makes sure the seller whose name is on the contract is the legal owner. They identify all the liens, mortgages, judgments, restrictions, easements, status of property taxes, and public assessments that must be satisfied before clear title can be conveyed to the buyer.

They keep in close contact with realtors, attorneys, and funding sources to assemble all the documents needed to close. They compile all the charges, miscellaneous fees, title company fees, and other closing costs into a final settlement statement. They will inform the buyer of the amount of money to bring for the closing. They require certified funds. The title company collects all funds necessary for the disbursement of funds to the parties involved. After closing, the title company will file the legal documents and make sure all outstanding liens have been paid.

In day trading, it is very important that your title company is comfortable with creative financing like options, flex options, assignments, and simultaneous closings. You also want responsive title searches. If they can't give you a title search in two days, then find another title company. The small shops are the best. They'll be more willing to work with investors, and you'll get better service.

And don't let them sell you a title insurance policy. This is only necessary if you are going to keep the house. But you are a day trader. You are only going to own the house for a few hours before selling. Your buyer/investor will purchase the title insurance.

Find Title Companies

You should find a title company that you can trust to handle this complex procedure efficiently and in accordance with the wishes of all the parties involved. The quality of their service is of utmost importance. Some places to look for title companies include:

- *Yellow Pages:* You'll find many good title companies in your local Yellow Pages. Call them all and make sure they can do a title search in no more than two days and are flexible enough to do creative closes, such as assignments and simultaneous closings.
- *Online searches:* Search "title and escrow services your city" or "title companies your city." Also try searching these directories for title companies in your area: (1) Open Directory (www.dmoz.org/Business/Real_Estate/Legal/Title_Services/Settlement_and_Escrow) and (2) Google Directory (www.google.com/Top/Business/Real_Estate/Legal/Title_Services/Settlement_and_Escrow). Add all the companies your find to your database, for follow-ups. Add these to your bookmarks under Real Estate Services.
- *Networking:* When looking for professional services like title companies ask the members of your online and offline investor groups and social networking sites for referrals.

HOME INSPECTION SERVICES
Find a Good Home Inspection Service

If you are dealing with a house that needs a lot of repairs, you should order a home inspection as well as a contractor inspection. Sometimes the home inspection service will uncover something your contractors missed. A home inspection is going to cost you about $300. But in the case of a possible problem house, it is well worth the extra cost. You're buying broken houses, as is. If there are any serious problems with the house that would result in higher repair costs you want to know about them before you close.

A thorough home inspection will give you the information you need to make a wise buying decision. Home inspection reports cover all the systems and components of a residential building such as HVAC, plumbing, electrical, foundation, roof, masonry structure, and exterior and interior components. If there is anything wrong, a home inspection will find it. Home inspection services are held liable for the information they report. That's why the best ones are covered by errors and omission insurance policies. Here are some places to find home inspection services:

- *Yellow Pages:* Start your search with the Yellow Pages.
- *Online searches:* Search "home inspectors your city" or "home inspection services your city." Also try searching Homegauge.com, Homecheck.com, and Alamode.com.
- *Networking:* Talk to your realtors and other members of your local real estate association. There are probably lots of home inspection services involved in these groups. And don't forget to use your social networking sites and online real estate groups to obtain referrals.

Prescreen Home Inspection Services

Most states require home inspectors to meet certain standards of practice, licensing, and educational requirements in order to inspect a home. If you live in a state that requires home inspectors to be licensed, then ask your home inspector to fax you his or her license. This shows that the home inspector has had some training and has passed a competency test.

Also ask your home inspector to supply documents showing his or her professional standards. The most common are from the American Society of Home Inspectors or the National Association of Home Inspectors.

Look for someone who is smart and thorough. Houses are complex structures, and you need a smart cookie to go in and identify critical issues. Make sure you are comfortable with the intelligence, credentials, and experience of your home inspector.

Finally, be sure your home inspector carries errors and omissions insurance. This insurance costs a lot. But having this insurance is a sign of professionalism. As well as protecting the inspector, it gives you the peace of mind that you are working with a professional.

REAL ESTATE ATTORNEYS PROTECT YOUR BACK

As previously mentioned, some states use attorneys and some use title companies. You need an attorney to prepare your documents and close the deal for you.

When you hire an attorney or title company, you don't even have to show up at the closing. I know that many of you have never used an attorney in your life. But do it now. And get used to it. Once you get started in day trading, attorneys will be a big part of your life. If you live in a state that uses title companies, they usually have attorneys on staff to handle your closing.

But don't give them too much responsibility. Their job is to do closings for you, point out legal issues you might not be aware of, and take care of all the paperwork for you. They are not there to make decisions for you, run your business, or give you financial advice. You can't wait until the last minute to find an attorney. You've got to do it now, before you're making deals. Once you start buying and selling houses, it will slow you down to hold everything up while you go out and interview attorneys.

Find a Good Real Estate Attorney

It's not hard to find real estate attorneys. A few places to look include:

- *Yellow Pages:* Many real estate attorneys are listed in the Yellow Pages by specialty. Flip to the real estate section, and you'll have dozens of attorneys to add to your database.
- *Online searches:* Search "real estate attorneys your city." Also try searching these directories: Alamode.com, Homegauge.com, and Homecheck.com.

  Search the Google Directory at Google.com and then drill down as follows: Top > Society > Law > Services > Lawyers and Law Firms > Property Law and Real Estate > North America > United States > Your State. Or drill down this way: Society > Law > Services > Lawyers and Law Firms > Property Law and Real Estate > North America > United States > Your State.
- *Networking:* Go to your real estate association and ask around for a good real estate attorney that everybody uses. Or go online and post an inquiry to your online real estate user group and write to your social networks. You'll find lots of attorneys to add to your database.

Use your database of realtors to deliver names of good real estate lawyers. I use my realtor autoresponder series to ask realtors to reply with referrals to good real estate attorneys. You can do the same thing. If the same name keeps coming up, then that's your guy or gal.

Prescreen Real Estate Attorneys

What do you look for in an attorney? First, make sure you're dealing with an attorney who spends at least 60 percent of his or her time on real estate, especially one who does a lot of residential closings. You don't want to have someone learn real estate law on your nickel, so make darn sure your candidates have at least five years of experience doing real estate deals.

It is a very good sign if they are recommended by other real estate investors or are themselves members of your local real estate association. That means that they have several full-time, professional real estate investors as clients. And it's great if they invest in real estate themselves.

Focus on attorneys who work for themselves or are partners in a small firm. Avoid the big law firms. You're too small for them. They'll never meet your individual needs and will most likely overcharge you. Attorneys running their own business will understand you better. And they might even cut you some slack on the fees. They are their own bosses and aren't pressured by upper management to charge more and do less.

In my opinion, lawyers who run their own practices probably have mindsets that are closer to a businessperson's mindset because they are running their own businesses, too. They are more flexible and willing to work with you on price and more. They don't have to answer to managing partners or hoards of other partners demanding certain profit margins.

Make sure your attorney is willing to listen to you about creative transactions like lease options, simultaneous closings, assignments, and holding your deposits in escrow instead of sending them to the listing agent. You don't want an attorney who starts preaching about why all of this stuff won't work.

Most of all you want someone who is responsive and will make things happen quickly and efficiently. You don't want an attorney who is dragging his or her feet and slowing things down.

No matter how experienced attorneys are, if they ignore you, they are not worth your money. They should be willing to answer simple questions without charging you. Find someone you like. If you don't enjoy interacting with them, don't hire them. You're paying the bill. So you get to choose who you work with.

The fee is not the major concern. If you find an attorney who will work for you and is experienced, competent, and responsive, that attorney is worth his or her weight in gold. Build the legal expenses into your property analysis. Then don't worry about it. It's just another cost of doing business. If you find a lawyer who will work with you on price, don't insult them by pushing too far. Remember, a good attorney doesn't need you, but you need them. Think of the cost as an investment in building your business for the long term.

CHAPTER 9

RISK-FREE, WIN-WIN, SIMPLE CONTRACTS: STRUCTURE BUYING AND SELLING CONTRACTS TO MAKE YOUR DEALS RISK FREE

No matter who you're dealing with or what they promise, you don't have anything until you have signatures in ink on paper. A contract is really the only thing that ensures that your sellers and buyers do what they say they will do. It is also the only line of defense you have if you don't see eye to eye with your seller, which happens in real estate.

Real estate contracts come in all shapes and sizes and use differing language that basically describes the same thing—an exchange of property between a seller and a buyer. Though these contracts are similar, a few carefully placed clauses can make a huge difference to your day trading business. In this chapter, I explain the basic contracts used while day trading houses. I tell you about three special clauses you should insert that realtors and owners/sellers accept that are critical to your success as a day trader. And I explain the contracts you should use when you are selling to your buyers/investors.

CONTRACTS FOR BUYING THROUGH REALTORS

When making an offer on a property through a realtor, the realtor will provide a standard form. Realtors expect you to use their form. If you come up with a contract of your own and try to get your realtor to use it, it will make you look bad and raise a lot of red flags. If you want to deal with realtors, you've got to use their forms.

CONTRACTS FOR BUYING FROM OWNERS/SELLERS

If you are buying from an owner/seller, you can still use the standard contract that realtors in your state use. Simply take the realtor logo off the document because no realtor is involved. Realtors throughout the state have fought tooth and nail about the provisions in these contracts and have considered all the issues. The contract they use is well thought out and very professional. You might as well use it for your closings.

Some real estate experts teach their students to use a simple one-page agreement for owners/sellers because the contract is legal and covers all the bases. They reason that because it is a legal contract read and signed voluntarily by the seller, it will hold up in court. But from a practical standpoint, if you write a simple contract with clauses that favor you, it could be a problem in court.

If you end up being sued over a contract in court, the first thing the judge will ask is "Who drafted this document?" And if you wrote the contract yourself, it won't look good in the eyes of the court. And the court might question your intentions in not using the standard state contract.

You also want your sellers to be comfortable with the form they are signing. If you write up your own contract, they might question it and feel insecure about signing it. However, if you use the standard form that every realtor in your area uses, you can tell them it's a standard form. If they check with their attorney and you are using the realtor-type form, then the attorney will confirm, "this is the same form that every realtor in the state uses." This gives sellers a great degree of comfort that they won't get from custom-made agreements. Be sure to check with your local attorney to make sure you can use the same agreement that the realtors use if you remove the logo. You don't want to do anything wrong, so just check with them first. And if you have to edit the form, let your attorney make any changes before you use it.

I believe firmly in full disclosure. For example, in the standard agreement that I use and that most realtors use, a reference is made to assignments, which explains that any assignment must be agreed on by both parties in a separate agreement. Truett Cathy, the founder of Chick-fil-A, Inc., has an enlightened mission statement that I admire. "Put people and principles before profits. And when you do that everyone profits." We have adopted that as our mission statement as well. Truett Cathy's Chick-fil-A is the only fast-food restaurant I know of that is closed on Sunday. That should tell you something.

You can use an assignment when you are dealing with sellers/owners. An assignment gives you permission to assign the rights to buy the property at a certain specified price to another party. In some cases you will want the right to assign the purchase of the house to your buyer/investor directly without closing on the house yourself. This will save you the cost of a second closing.

If you present this clearly to sellers in a sincere way, most will understand and accept your assignment provisions. Just explain that an associate of yours might want to take part in the transaction. And if this is the case, you need to be able to assign the contract to him or her. Actually what difference does it make to a seller who is actually closing on the property as long as the conditions in the contract are met? More about assignments later.

To find a copy of the standard contract that realtors in your state use, you can get online and go to Google and type in the words "realtor contract your state" or "real estate contract your state" or "real estate purchase agreement your state." You can also do an advanced search on Google by selecting only PDF files in your search. This way you will only get search results that are PDF files. This will help you find what you are looking for much faster. Be sure to have your attorney check over the document you downloaded to make sure it is proper for you to use. You could also ask one of your realtors for a copy.

CLAUSES IN CONTRACTS TO BUY PROPERTIES

There are numerous clauses that you can use in a contract. However, I suggest that you keep it simple. As I mentioned before, if you are using a realtor, or you are buying a property that is listed with a realtor, then you use the realtor's contract form.

That said, there are some very important clauses you must have if you are going to be successful in day trading. You need to make offers fast and with utmost confidence. To make offers confidently without ever seeing the property, you must have clauses in your contracts that make it easy for you to break the contracts if you wish, without any repercussions or financial loss. You don't want to overburden your contracts with too many clauses. Sellers will notice and might refuse your contract. Here are some valuable clauses that will benefit you enormously and that most sellers will never have a problem with.

Must-Have Clauses in Contracts with Sellers

When we buy property there are three short, but very important clauses that we should put in our contracts:

1. *This contract is subject to a 15-day inspection and approval of the condition of the property.* This is the time we need to get the contractor to inspect the property and estimate repairs and the appraiser to give us an after-repair value appraisal. Even if an inspection clause is in the contract, you still need to write it in.

2. *This contract is subject to an acceptable appraisal.* This lets the seller know that we are not paying the value of the property but that we want an acceptable appraisal. We have even had some of them say, "What do you mean by acceptable?" You could tell them that you will let them know when the appraisal comes in whether or not it is acceptable. We do not usually get any resistance with this.

3. *The deposit shall be the sole remedy in the event of buyers default.* If you received your inspection and the repairs were more than expected and you forgot to let the seller or realtor know within 15 days, then the most you can lose is your deposit. This covers you in the event that you cannot close. The most you could lose is your deposit, which is usually about $500. But if the inspection comes in too high or the appraisal comes in too low, you will try to renegotiate with your seller or realtor.

As a general rule, outside of these three clauses, you don't need anything else.

One Clause That You Do Not Need

One clause that realtors and buyers hate is a financing contingency. Because you have your own cash or source of cash from your own credit or day trading funder, you don't need a financing contingency. When realtors see this they light up and get real happy. It means that a big payday for them is not far off. You have the funds. And all you're asking for is a few days to inspect the property and get an appraisal. These are very reasonable requests. And realtors will understand why you need them. They would ask for time to appraise and inspect the property if they were buying it themselves. It's simply being prudent.

And because you're not asking for a financing contingency, you are acting like a cash buyer should be acting. It creates a very good impression. You will get a lot more of your offers accepted, approved, and closed if you do not put any sort of financing contingency in your offer. And, with these other three clauses, you do not have to worry about it anyway. You have your out in the event that you need one.

CONTRACTS FOR SELLING TO INVESTORS

Everything I said previously applies to consumer transactions and realtor transactions. A consumer transaction is basically a transaction where you are either buying from someone who lives in a property or selling to someone who will be living in the property.

You will want to use your own form and make sure your buyer/investor does his or her own due diligence. Or at least you cover yourself by telling them in writing to do so.

When you're dealing with buyers/investors, you want to offer your properties at a specific listed price that is nonnegotiable. You have no room in your instant property analysis to accommodate a reduction in price. When someone submits an offer on one of your houses, ask for an earnest deposit with the contract and addendums. I usually ask for $500 to $2,000 depending on the price of the house.

I always ask for twice the amount of the deposit that I paid. If I paid a $500 deposit to the seller, I ask my buyer for $1,000. Then if the deal falls through, I have at least doubled my deposit money.

My investor sales agreement is nothing like the standard sales agreement used by realtors in dealing with consumers. Our attorney designed this contract specifically for our purposes while day trading houses. Don't use our contract verbatim. Use it as a guide to preparing your own. Have your attorney look it over and modify it for your needs, according to the laws within your state. Here are some of the key clauses we've included:

- *"Buyer warrants that they are purchasing the property for use as an investment and not as a personal residence."* I want to clarify up front that I am dealing with an investor and not an owner/occupant.

- "*Buyer cannot advertise or promote the property prior to close.*" and "*Possession of said premises will be given to purchaser at the time of closing.*" I don't want my buyers to start acting as a buyer until they close. The reasons are obvious. I have not yet closed on the property myself. I only have it under contract, and the seller does not permit anyone to advertise or in any way act as an owner until after closing.
- "*This contract is not assignable.*" I want buyers/investors who have the funds and are ready to buy immediately. I don't want buyers who are going to wholesale the property to someone else while the clock is ticking on the deal and I'm running out of time.
- "*This contract is subject to a 48-hour inspection period upon acceptance of offer.*" As a real estate day trader, my time is short. I have done the inspection for the buyer and gotten an appraisal. I want buyers who are willing to move fast because I've done a lot of the due diligence for them. Forty-eight hours to inspect the property is adequate.
- "*Seller agrees to deliver premises at time of closing in an as-is condition.*" This lets the buyer know that there are no warranties. They are hereby notified that they are purchasing this house as is.
- "*If the closing does not occur by the Closing Date, the Agreement is automatically terminated and the Seller shall retain any earnest money deposit as liquidated damages.*" This protects the buyer from having to buy the house if they decide not to close. This is why it is a good idea to have one or two backup buyers in case your first buyer drops out at the last minute.
- "*In the event Buyer requests an extension of the Closing Date or of the deadline for the fulfillment of any contingency, and the Seller agrees to the extension, the Buyer agrees to pay to the Seller a per diem penalty of the greater of $50.00 or 0.1 of 1 percent of the purchase price per calendar day toward Seller's carrying costs, through and including the Closing Date specified in the written extension agreement. The per diem amount must be deposited with the Seller at the time any request for extension is made.*" This keeps buyers from wasting your time by requesting frivolous extensions they do not seriously plan to follow through on.
- "*Seller agrees to deliver a good and marketable or insurable owner's title to the property above described free and clear of all encumbrances except as herein set forth.*" This assures the buyer that you have done a title search and to your knowledge the title is clear or will be clear by closing. Your attorney or title company will do this for you.
- "*Purchaser agrees to notify Seller in writing of any defects in title as soon as reasonably possible and if title proves to be not good and marketable or insurable, the seller is to make title good and marketable or insurable and shall*

have reasonable time from notification so to do." If an encumbrance on the property becomes known to the buyer after the closing, they have recourse to come back to you, the seller, and get the title cleared. It also puts the buyer on notice that they have to make this request to you in writing and give you time to respond.

- *"Buyer shall pay for state and county documentary stamps and preparation of deed."* These are the closing costs that the buyer is required to pay.

Addendums to Contracts of Sale

We also ask our buyers/investors to sign two addendums to the contract of sale. The first one asks the buyer/investor to acknowledge in writing that they understand they are purchasing the property in its existing condition without any representation or warranties of any kind or nature.

It explains that the buyer has been given a reasonable opportunity to inspect and investigate the property either independently or through agents of buyer's choosing at buyer's expense. With this addendum, the buyer also affirms that in purchasing the property, he or she is not relying on you, the seller, as to the condition of the property:

- *"Buyer acknowledges in that they understand they are purchasing the property in its existing condition without any representation or warranties of any kind or nature. Buyer also affirms that in purchasing the property, he or she is not relying on you, the seller, as to the condition of the property."*

The second addendum basically applies to buyer financing through our sister company, Financial Help Services, Inc.:

- *"If the Buyer chooses to use Financial Help Services, Inc. for financing and closing is delayed or cancelled because of financing, all stipulations of this contract and addendum still apply as if any other lender were financing the property for the Buyer."* This means the buyer cannot use the fact they were turned down by our sister company for financing as an excuse to void the provisions of the sales contact they signed with us.
- *"If financing is not provided by Financial Help Services, Inc., then proof of funds are required at time of acceptance."* Before accepting the contract we must know where the funds are going to come from.
- *"Any loan application fees, appraisal fees, credit report fees, inspection fees, surveys or legal fees incurred or paid for by the Purchaser are incurred or paid at the risk of the Purchaser and may not be refundable."* That means that if the buyer/investor cannot close he or she is still responsible for the due diligence expenses that were incurred.

- *"Seller cannot warrant or guarantee that the property, the transaction, and/or borrower is financeable now or in the future."* If a buyer decides to apply to our sister company for financing we cannot guarantee they will be able to obtain financing.
- *"The contract is subject to the Seller being able to acquire the property, if not closed yet."* This is important if you're a day trader. You will be buying and then selling in the same day. This lets the buyer know that you may not have closed on the property yourself yet. This is another example of full disclosure.
- *"Buyer expressly waives the remedy of specific performance in the event seller is unable to convey title."* The buyer cannot sue you if you cannot deliver the property with a clear title.
- *"Buyer waives right to record a lis pendens against the property or to record the agreement or memorandum thereof in the real property records."* This contract by itself does not give the buyer any right to encumber the property's title prior to closing.
- *"Buyer waives right to invoke any other equitable remedy that may be available that, if invoked, would prevent the Seller from conveying the property to a third-party buyer."* This means if my buyer backs out of the deal, he or she will not create any cloud on the title preventing me from selling the property.

I have put the current contract package that we use when people buy houses from us on the next few pages and on our web site at www.RealEstateDayTrading.com in the forms section for you to download and edit any way you want. Once you edit it the way you want, you will want to create a PDF version so if you put it on your web site or e-mail it to a potential buyer they cannot edit it. I put all of my documents into one PDF document and put it on our buying and selling web site so the buyer can simply download it and fill it out and fax it back to us to make the offer on our property. If you want to receive notices of our properties as they become available, you may want to go to www.InvestorsRehab.com and sign up.

You can also submit a property to us there as well. In fact, if you have a property you want us to look at, please do not call or e-mail, instead, submit it at www.InvestorsRehab.com. And if you would like an editable version of our contract package to use for yourself, you can get it by going to www.RealEstateDayTrading.com/Bonuses. Figures 9.1 through 9.4 are the contract package we currently use.

Investors Rehab, Inc.
4341 Charlotte Hwy Suite 211
P.O. Box 5261
Lake Wylie, SC 29710
803-831-0056
Fax 803-831-0805

To submit an offer, please submit the attached contract and addendum. You must also submit the correct deposit for your offer and contract to be complete.

The required deposit is listed on the property details page. To insure your deposit is received in a timely manner you may wish to pay your deposit with a credit card directly from the property listing page on our web site. If you elect to send your deposit, we suggest using overnight or priority service to insure receipt. You can send it to the address listed above.

Unless your offer is all cash you need to either be approved with FHS or submit proof of funds or approval letter with the offer.

To view a property, please contact the appropriate person with Investors Rehab, Inc. to make arrangements to obtain access.

Most of our properties are sold in less than two (2) hours. We do however take backup contracts.

You can use any attorney you want; however, it may save you time and money to use the same attorney we used to buy the property. They may or may not have been recommended by the seller or real estate agent.

You also may be able to use an existing appraisal obtained by Investors Rehab; however, depending on your lender or your preference, you may need an additional appraisal.

Because of the deep discounted prices we have negotiated on the properties we resell to investors and the small margins we work off of, we are unable to negotiate on the prices offered. We provide real values and discounted prices on the wholesale properties we offer.

We will be glad to refer any contractors, appraisers, attorneys, property managers, etc. if we are aware of any in the area of the property; however, you must interview them and make your own decision about relying on their information or services. We highly recommend getting detailed descriptions in writing with any vendor used.

Because we usually buy and sell our properties on the same day it is extremely important for you to close on the anticipated closing date in your contract to avoid penalties.

We take each and every offer very seriously.

All offers are subject to prior sales and withdrawals.

Once you have completed the contract and addendum please fax them back to 803-831-0805.

Copyright © 2009 by Larry Goins. To customize this document, download Figure 9.1 to your hard drive from www.realestatedaytrading.com/bonuses. The document can then be opened, edited, and printed using Microsoft Word or another popular word processing application.

FIGURE 9.1   Instructions for Submitting an Offer

Investors Rehab, Inc.
4341 Charlotte Highway, Suite 211
Lake Wylie SC 29710
(803) 831-0056 office (803) 831-0805 fax

This is a legally binding contract entered into this day _____. RECEIPT IS HEREBY ACKNOWLEDGED OF THE SUM OF: _____ Dollars ($_____) From _____ (Buyer) as a deposit on account of the purchase price of the following described property upon the terms and conditions as stated herein. DESCRIPTION OF PROPERTY: That lot, piece, or parcel of land situated in _____ County, State of _____ Carolina. Address _____ City _____ State _____ Zip _____ For the PURCHASE PRICE of: _____Dollars ($_____)

TERMS AND CONDITIONS OF SALE: _____
_____
_____

Buyer warrants that they are purchasing the property for use as an investment and not as a personal residence.

Buyer cannot advertise or promote the property prior to close.

Possession of said premises will be given to purchaser at the time of closing.

This contract is not assignable.

Taxes, rent and rent securities shall be prorated at the time of closing and paid by the seller.

This contract is subject to a 48-hour inspection period upon acceptance of offer.

Seller agrees to deliver premises at time of closing in an as-is condition. In case the property is destroyed, wholly or partially, by fire or other casualty prior to closing, Buyer or Seller shall have option for ten (10) days thereafter of proceeding or terminating agreement.

Said property is being sold and purchased subject to zoning ordinances and regulations; building restrictions; and conditions, restrictions and easements of Public Record.

It is agreed that time is of the essence with respect to all dates specified in the Agreement and any addenda, riders, or amendments thereto. This means that all deadlines are intended to be strict and absolute. If the closing does not occur by the Closing Date, the Agreement is automatically terminated and the Seller shall retain any earnest money deposit as liquidated damages.

FIGURE 9.2   Contract of Sale

In the event Buyer requests an extension of the Closing Date or of the deadline for the fulfillment of any contingency, and the Seller agrees to the extension, the Buyer agrees to pay to the Seller a per diem penalty of the greater of $50.00 or 1/10 of 1% of the purchase price per calendar day towards Seller's carrying costs, through and including the Closing Date specified in the written extension agreement. The per diem amount must be deposited with the Seller at the time any request for extension is made.

Seller agrees to deliver a good and marketable or insurable owner's title to the property above described free and clear of all encumbrances except as herein set forth. Buyer shall pay for state and county documentary stamps and preparation of deed. Purchaser agrees to notify Seller in writing of any defects in title as soon as reasonably possible and if title proves to be not good and marketable or insurable, the seller is to make title good and marketable or insurable and shall have a reasonable time from notification so to do. The Buyer and Seller have until, _____, _____ to accept this Offer to Purchase and Contract of Sale and if not returned then contract shall be null and void and of no force and effect.

This transaction shall be closed, the balance of the moneys due shall be paid, and all documents signed by the parties hereto on or before _____, _____.
The deposit is to be held by the Seller pending closing. It is expressly agreed that upon the event of any default or failure on the part of the Purchaser to comply with the terms and conditions of this contract that said deposit is to be paid to Seller as liquidated damages.

The parties hereto further agree that this written contract and the attached Addendum expresses the entire agreement between the parties and that there is no other agreement, oral or otherwise, modifying the terms hereunder.

This contract shall be binding on both parties, their principles, heirs, personal representatives, or assigns. It is agreed that the listing broker in this transaction, if any, is _____ and the selling broker in this transaction, if any, is _____.

The undersigned jointly and severally agree to purchase and sell the above-described property on the terms and conditions stated in the foregoing instrument and attached addendum that must be attached and included as part of this contract.

PURCHASER (S)	Date	SELLER (S)	Date
_____	_____	_____	_____
_____	_____	_____	_____
WITNESSES:	Date	WITNESSES:	Date
_____	_____	_____	_____
_____	_____	_____	_____

This is a legally binding contract. If not understood, seek the advice of an Attorney.

FIGURE 9.2   *(Continued)*

Investors Rehab, Inc.
4341 Charlotte Highway, Suite 211
Lake Wylie SC 29710
(803) 831-0056 office (803) 831-0805 fax

Controlled Business Disclosure, Hold Harmless and As Is –Where Is Addendum
Address _____ **City** _____ **State** _____
Buyer is purchasing the property in its **"EXISTING CONDITION," WITHOUT REPRESEN-TATION OR WARRANTIES OF ANY KIND OR NATURE**. Buyer acknowledges for buyer and buyer's successors, heirs, and assignees that buyer has been given a reasonable opportunity to inspect and investigate the property and all improvements thereon, either independently or through agents of buyer's choosing at buyer's expense and that in purchasing the property, Buyer is not relying on Seller or Seller's Agent, as to the condition of the property and/orany improvements thereon, including but not necessarily limited to, **ALL EXISTING WINDOW COVERINGS, FLOOR COVERINGS, ELECTRICAL, PLUMBING, HEATING, SEWAGE, SEPTIC, ROOF, FOUNDATION, SOILS AND GEOLOGY, LOT SIZE OR SUITABILITY OF THE PROPERTY AND/OR ITS IMPROVEMENTS FOR PARTICULAR PURPOSES, OR THAT THE IMPROVEMENTS ARE STRUCTURALLY SOUND AND/OR IN COMPLIANCE WITH ANY CITY, COUNTY, STATE AND/OR FEDERAL CODES OR ORDINANCES**. Buyer also acknowledges that the Seller makes no promises, guarantees, representations, or warranties, either expressed or implied, as to the present or future market value of the subject property, encroachments, easements, or profitability nor the presence or absence of any hazardous or toxic substances or contamination including but not limited to: radon, lead, electromagnetic radiation, mold, mildew, microscopic organisms, lead paint, fuel oil, allergens, or asbestos, whether known or unknown and whether or not such defects or conditions were discoverable through inspection.

Buyer and Seller both waive the right to Seller's disclosure form, if applicable.

Seller does not warrant existing structure as to its habitability or suitability for occupancy. BUYER(S) ASSUMES RESPONSIBILITY TO CHECK THE APPROPRIATE PLANNING AUTHORITY FOR INTENDED USE AND HOLDS SELLER AND BROKER HARMLESS AS TO THE SUITABILITY FOR BUYER(S) INTENDED USE.

Buyer(s) further states that they are relying solely upon their own inspections of subject property and not upon any representation made to them by any person whomsoever, and is purchasing the subject property in the condition in which it now is, without any obligation on the part of the Seller to make any changes, alterations, repairs, or future obligations of any nature whatsoever.

FIGURE 9.3   Investor's Rehab

Any report (s) that is required by the Buyer's Lender is to be the sole responsibility of the Buyer. Buyer shall neither make nor cause to be made: (i) invasive or destructive investigations; or (ii) inspections by any governmental building or zoning inspector or government employee, unless required by Law. Buyer is not allowed to perform, order, or otherwise cause any repair(s) and/or work to be done on the property prior to closing.

When visiting or inspecting the property, Buyer's and Buyer's Representative enter the premises at their own risk, and Seller shall not be liable for any injuries, or damage suffered or incurred, to any Buyer's or Buyer's Representatives person or personal property, as a result of such entry.

The undersigned, Buyer, acting personally and for their representatives, affiliates, and/or organization, if any, each hereby agrees to defend, indemnify, and hold harmless Investors Rehab, Inc., Financial Help Services, Inc., and any parent or affiliate and all shareholders, employees, officers, and directors from and against any and all claims, demands, suits, actions, damages, judgments, cost, charges, and expenses including, without limitation, court cost and attorneys fees, of any nature whatsoever that any such, buyer and/or their affiliate, representative, or organization may suffer, sustain, or incur resulting from, arising out of, or in any way connected with any action taken by, or inaction on the part of, any buyer or their affiliate, representative, or organization in connection with this transaction.

Information given to the Buyer may not have been verified by the Seller and is not guaranteed to be accurate. The Buyer should not rely on such information in deciding to purchase property. It is the Buyer's responsibility to conduct his own inspections to verify any information, including square footage, provided to him. Should the Buyer rely on advice or representations made by Seller in deciding to purchase said property, Buyer is doing so at his own risk.

It is the policy of the Seller to make no promises, guarantees, representations, or warranties, either expressed or implied. If any expressed or implied promises, guarantees, representations, or warranties were made, they should be disregarded.

If the property was built before 1978, the Buyer acknowledges receipt of a lead-based paint brochure and disclosure available on the web site, www.InvestorsRehab.com and must sign and attach the lead-based paint disclosure as part of this contract and addendum.

Seller recommends that Purchaser obtain a survey and plat of the property.

If financial services are provided by Financial Help Services, Inc., a conflict of interest exists. An officer and shareholder of Financial Help Services, Inc. is also an officer of Investors Rehab, Inc. The buyer may seek alternate sources for financial services if desired.

FIGURE 9.3   (*Continued*)

If Buyer chooses to use Financial Help Services, Inc. for financing and closing is delayed or cancelled because of financing, all stipulations of this contract and addendum still apply as if any other lender were financing the property for the Buyer.

If financing is not provided by Financial Help Services, Inc., then proof of funds are required at time of acceptance.

Any loan application fees, appraisal fees, credit report fees, inspection fees, survey or legal fees incurred or paid for by the Purchaser are incurred or paid at the risk of the Purchaser and may not be refundable.

Seller cannot warrant or guarantee that the property, the transaction, and/or borrower is financeable now or in the future.

Seller acknowledges they are buying or have recently bought this property in its "As Is" condition without representation or warranties, and without personal inspection, and are relying on third parties to inspect and appraise the property and investment as a whole.

The contract is subject to the Seller being able to acquire the property, if not closed yet.

Buyer expressly waives the remedy of specific performance in the event seller is unable to convey title.

Buyer waives right to record a lis pendens against the property or to record the agreement or memorandum thereof in the real property records.

Buyer waives right to invoke any other equitable remedy that may be available that, if invoked, would prevent the Seller from conveying the property to a third-party buyer.

Seller reserves the right to continue to offer Property for sale until this offer has been formally accepted in writing and all contingencies removed in writing.

Buyer **ACKNOWLEDGES** that since the exact figures for property taxes may be unknown at this time, we understand that the tax Prorations on the settlement statement may be based on estimates or the prior year's taxes. In the event that taxes were paid for the preceding year on unimproved basis, the Prorations are based on estimates for the current year. In the event that taxes for the proceeding year were paid on improved basis and the exact current tax amounts are unavailable, Prorations are based on amounts for the preceding year. It is understood that there **WILL BE NO ADJUSTMENTS** made between seller and purchaser after closing. We do further agree that Prorations as reflected on the attached settlement statement are accept-able, and by signature hereon each party agrees to hold each other harmless from any tax or other adjustments in the future.

Inspection examinations, certifications, appraisals, research, closings, repair estimates, repairs, or other services may be performed by vendors or contractors selected or recom-mended by Seller as a convenience to the parties. Buyer agrees to hold harmless the Sellers as to the performance or nonperformance and costs of such vendors or contrac-tors and is using such vendor or information obtained by such vendors at their own risk.

FIGURE 9.3   (*Continued*)

The undersigned agrees that they have the full authority to execute this document personally and for any organization they represent or will represent. By signing you agree that you have read, understand, and have the full power and authority to enter into this legal agreement. If you do not understand this document please seek legal counsel prior to signing. The undersigned acknowledges receipt of a copy of this document.

In the event there is any conflict between this addendum and the contract, the terms of this addendum take precedence and shall prevail, except as otherwise provided by applicable law.

The **CLOSING OF THIS TRANSACTION** shall constitute as acknowledgment by the Buyer(s) that **THE PREMISES WERE ACCEPTED WITHOUT REPRESENTATION OR WARRANTY OF ANY KIND OR NATURE AND IN ITS PRESENT "AS IS" CONDITION BASED SOLELY ON BUYER'S OWN INSPECTION**.

_____   _____

Buyer Signature   Date

_____   _____

Name

_____   _____

Buyer Signature   Date

_____   _____

Name

Copyright © 2009 by Larry Goins. To customize this document, download Figure 9.3 to your hard drive from www.realestatedaytrading.com/bonuses. The document can then be opened, edited, and printed using Microsoft Word or another popular word processing application.

FIGURE 9.3   (*Continued*)

Investors Rehab, Inc.
4341 Charlotte Highway, Suite 211
Lake Wylie, SC 29710
(803) 831-0056 office (803) 831-0805 fax

If Buyer chooses to use Financial Help Services, Inc. for financing and closing is delayed or cancelled because of financing, all stipulations of this contract and addendum still apply as if any other lender were financing the property for the Buyer.

If financing is not provided by Financial Help Services, Inc., then proof of funds are required at time of acceptance.

Any loan application fees, appraisal fees, credit report fees, inspection fees, survey or legal fees incurred or paid for by the Purchaser are incurred or paid at the risk of the Purchaser and may not be refundable.

Seller cannot warrant or guarantee that the property, the transaction, and/or borrower is financeable now or in the future.

Seller acknowledges they are buying or have recently bought this property in its "As Is" condition without representation or warranties, and without personal inspection, and are relying on third parties to inspect and appraise the property and investment as a whole.

The contract is subject to the Seller being able to acquire the property, if not closed yet.

Buyer expressly waives the remedy of specific performance in the event seller is unable to convey title.

Buyer waives right to record a lis pendens against the property or to record the agreement or memorandum thereof in the real property records.

Buyer waives right to invoke any other equitable remedy that may be available that, if invoked, would prevent the Seller from conveying the property to a third-party buyer.

Seller reserves the right to continue to offer Property for sale until this offer has been formally accepted in writing and all contingencies removed in writing.

Buyer **ACKNOWLEDGES** that since the exact figures for property taxes may be unknown at this time, we understand that the tax Prorations on the settlement statement may be based on estimates or the prior year's taxes. In the event that taxes were paid for the preceding year on unimproved basis, the Prorations are based on estimates for the current year. In the event that taxes for the proceeding year were paid on improved basis and the exact current tax amounts are unavailable, Prorations are based on amounts for the preceding year. It is

FIGURE 9.4   Addendum to Contract of Sale

understood that there **WILL BE NO ADJUSTMENTS** made between seller and purchaser after closing. We do further agree that Prorations as reflected on the attached settlement statement are acceptable, and by signature hereon each party agrees to hold each other harmless from any tax or other adjustments in the future.

Inspection examinations, certifications, appraisals, research, closings, repair estimates, repairs, or other services may be performed by vendors or contractors selected or recommended by Seller as a convenience to the parties. Buyer agrees to hold harmless the Sellers as to the performance or nonperformance and costs of such vendors or contractors and is using such vendor or information obtained by such vendors at their own risk.

The undersigned agrees that they have the full authority to execute this document personally and for any organization they represent or will represent. By signing you agree that you have read, understand, and have the full power and authority to enter into this legal agreement. If you do not understand this document please seek legal counsel prior to signing. The undersigned acknowledges receipt of a copy of this document.

In the event there is any conflict between this addendum and the contract, the terms of this addendum take precedence and shall prevail, except as otherwise provided by applicable law.

The **CLOSING OF THIS TRANSACTION** shall constitute as acknowledgment by the Buyer(s) that **THE PREMISES WERE ACCEPTED WITHOUT REPRESENTATION OR WARRANTY OF ANY KIND OR NATURE AND IN ITS PRESENT "AS IS" CONDITION BASED SOLELY ON BUYER'S OWN INSPECTION**.

_____   _____

Buyer Signature   Date

_____   _____

Name

_____   _____

Buyer Signature   Date

_____   _____

Name

FIGURE 9.4   (*Continued*)

CHAPTER 10

NEGOTIATION SCRIPTS AND TIPS FOR GETTING YOUR DEALS ACCEPTED

Now you have everything in place to start making offers. You've got your database of motivated buyers and seller. You've got your funding and the contracts you need to make offers. You just have to start doing it.

Remember, your goal is to make as many offers as you can that match your numbers. You know from your instant property analysis the most you can pay. You cannot exceed that amount. As long as you stay below the maximum amount, you can make offers confidently knowing that you will make money. Don't worry about any particular offer. It is merely a numbers game. Some offers will go through, some will be rejected. If you get one out of ten accepted you'll make a lot of money each month.

The question now is how do you negotiate those deals. What do you say to owners/sellers? What do you say to realty listing agents? Remember, deals are made, not found. You have to make your own deals. You do this by building rapport, getting people to like and trust you. When you become a real estate day trader, you will come into contact with all kinds of people in many different financial circumstances. But remember this, bad things sometimes happen to good people. So no matter what a person's situation, do not ever talk down to them or treat them like you are better than they are. People will forget what you said, but they will never forget how you made them feel. Please remember this.

WHAT TO SAY ON YOUR FIRST PHONE CALL TO OWNERS/SELLERS

Before you talk to any owners/sellers, be sure you have composed a script. Then become familiar and comfortable with it. Compose the script according to the guidelines I provide for you here. Keep this script in front of you at all times, especially when you're new at this business. Once you become very familiar with all the information in the script, then you can start asking the questions without having to look at the script.

You have to match the emotional attitude of the people you talk to. If they are relaxed and talk slow, then you talk slow. If they are excited and talk fast, then you talk fast. And remember you want to get your offer to them on the first phone call to get them "in the glue." That means they are excited to deal with you because you are serious enough to actually make an offer, not just talk.

Here are 12 steps you should include when developing your script:

1. *Introduce yourself.* The first thing you must do is introduce yourself and tell them why you are calling. Your goal then is to find out if the house is something you want to make an offer on and how much to offer. Always let the sellers try to sell you on their house. You want to get the sellers to start describing their house to you.

    "Hi. This is Larry Goins. I'm returning your phone call. You called me about a home that you have for sale. Could you tell me a little bit about it?"

2. *Get contact information.*

    "Before we continue talking, can you give me your contact information in case we're cut off? What is your name, address, e-mail address, and phone number?" Also ask for the following information when you have a chance: "What's your spouse's name? May we call you at work? What's the best time to call?"

3. *Ask about the house.* "What type of house is it—brick, wood frame, or stucco? When was it built? How many bedrooms, how many baths?" Ask: "What is the tax value? How many square feet? Are there any recent improvements? What is the square footage?"

4. *Ask about needed repairs.* These questions are the most important questions because they will enable you to do your instant property analysis.

    "Does it need to be repaired? What is the approximate cost of the needed repairs? Just a ballpark. What would the house sell for, assuming the repairs were made? Just a ballpark. How did you come up with that number?"

5. *Ask about financing.*

   "What is the amount of the first mortgage? How far behind are you? What is the amount of the second mortgage? How far behind are you? Are you in foreclosure? When is the foreclosure date? Are there any other liens?"

6. *Find out about ownership.*

   "Whose name is the house listed in? Is there anyone else making decisions? Who?"

7. *Set yourself up to make an offer.* These questions tend to amplify the sellers need to sell and excite their motivation to sell. This makes them more open to an offer from you, even if it is low. Don't ask these all at once. Just work them into your conversation.

   "Why are you selling? What will you do if you don't sell? How quickly do you want to sell? What else should I be asking?"

   "Are there any other problems with the house? What will you do with the money? Do you have any other property to sell?"

   "How long has it been for sale? Had any offers? How much? Why didn't you take it? Listed with realtor? How much?"

   "Vacant? How long? Rented? Rent amount? Tenants current?"

8. *Start negotiating the deal.* Be sure to ask this question with a strong yet friendly voice.

   "What is the least amount you can take if we close by Friday with all cash?"

9. *Persist and ask them for an amount another time.* Your seller may not be able to give you an amount at this time. If they can't, then follow up later.

10. *Explain who you are and how you work.*

    "Let me tell you a little about what we do. We buy houses, we pay cash, and we can close in about a week. The advantage of selling your home to someone like us, whether to me or any other investor, is that we can close fast and we pay all cash. So if you need to sell now and sell the property in its 'as is' condition, we can help you. What is the least amount you can take for your house if we can close by Friday?"

11. *Continue with the following, and give them an offer.* You want to try to get them to give you an offer first. But if they can't come up with a number, then you make an offer based on your instant property analysis.

    "In order to pay cash and close in about a week, we need to be able to buy a house around 60 to 65 percent of the market value. This is because when we buy a house we have to pay the taxes, insurance, upkeep, rehab costs, interest, and so on, we have to advertise it and show it, and it usually takes six to nine months to sell. We are looking for the buyer that you are looking for only we are willing to wait six to nine months. Based on what you told me about your house, we would probably need that to be around $32,867." (Remember to select a price that allows room for negotiation, roughly about 15 percent below your maximum allowable price.)

"Is that something that you think you could work with?" (The answer will always be no.)

Then ask, "How close could you come?"

12. *Prepare the purchase and sale agreement.* If you are dealing with owners/sellers and once they agree to a price that is below your maximum allowable price, make a nominal earnest money deposit of $10, no more.

WHAT TO SAY ON YOUR FIRST PHONE CALL TO REALTY LISTING AGENTS

Remember, if you want the realtor to call you back on the next property, then you need to make your offer exactly the way I show you. Also, when leaving a voice mail for a realtor to call you back about a property, it is important to tell them that you want to make an offer on one of their properties. This way you are assured they will call you back. After all, you will make your first offer on the first phone call. Before you talk to any realtors be sure you have composed a script for talking to them. Then become familiar and comfortable with it. Compose the script according to the guidelines I provide for you here in these fourteen steps:

1. *Get connected to the right listing agent.*

    "Hi, my name is Larry Goins, and I was calling about the property at _____ (address). Could you tell me who the listing agent is? _____ Great! May I speak with him/her?"

    "Not there? Oh, I don't have their cell number with me." Then just shut up, and wait a few seconds, and they will usually give the realtor's cell number to you. This lets them assume you do have it but just not with you.

2. *Introduce yourself to the listing agent when you get them on the phone.*

    "Hi, my name is Larry Goins, and I am an investor and I saw your listing at _____ (address). Could you tell me a little about it?"

3. *Ask about the property in a conversational manner.*
   "Number of bedrooms, number of baths, square feet, age, vacant, bank-owned?"

4. *Hone in on repair costs and after-appraised market value.*
   "How much work does it need? Just a ballpark estimate."
   "How much would it rent for? Just a ballpark estimate."
   "How's the market there? Would this be a good rental or is it better suited as retail property?"
   "What would it appraise for after repairs? Just a ballpark estimate."
   "Could you sell it for that once I fix it up? How long do you think it would it be on the market?"

5. *Help the realtor think about the difficulty he/she is having selling it now in its unrepaired state.*
   "Have you had any offers on this house? How long has it been on the market?"

6. *Go in for the close.*
   "I know you work for the seller, but I also know that you want to get this house sold. What do you think it would take to buy this house with an all cash offer? Do you work with many investors? As I mentioned, I'm an investor, and we buy houses and can pay cash and close fast."

7. *Build your credibility further with this question.*
   "If the property is bank-owned, could you ask the asset manager if the bank owns any more properties in the area? I may be interested in buying more than one property for a bigger discount."

8. *Make your offer.* This will really boost your credibility with the realtor. Most people are all show and no go.
   "Based on what you have told me, it looks like I need to be around $32,867. Do you think we should make an offer on this house?"
   (You have been running your numbers while on the phone using the instant property analysis, so you know what you can pay. Be sure to make the offer a little less than the maximum you can pay. If they say yes.)
   "Let's make an all cash offer of $32,867. Make it subject to an inspection with a 15-day extension. Do you need to submit the offer in writing or do you want to talk to the seller first?"

9. *If in writing, tell them to add this to the contract.*
   "The buyer is going to be 'Your Company Name' and/or assigns."

If they complain about the and/or assigns, tell them we never know what name we are going to title the property in until closing.

If they will not allow the assigns then just know that you will have to close this deal either by simultaneous closing or using one of your day funding sources.

10. *Ask about the deposit.*

"How much deposit do you need? Just fax me the contract, and I will sign it and send you a check."

Usually when you're dealing with houses listed with a realtor, you should make an earnest money deposit of about $500. It might be as low as $100. But don't deposit any more than $1,000.

11. *Always ask about other properties they are listing.*

"Do you have anything else I need to be looking at?"

12. *Give them your contact information.*

"By the way, do you mind if I get your e-mail address so we can stay in touch and I can buy some more property from you?" They will always give it to you.

"Thanks a lot and I look forward to working with you. Have a great day."

If your offer is not accepted (which is what usually happens), then you will have to negotiate back and forth until you seal the deal. But you have a good start by making an offer on the first phone call. Keep negotiating until you reach an agreement. But never exceed your maximum price. Remember, you will not get them all and it is a numbers game. The more offers you make the more will be accepted.

13. *Keep your name in front of them.* When presenting a written contract always put your phone number and contact information in the upper right corner of the contract. They may throw away your business card, but they will always hang on to the offer you made them.

14. *Always act like you have the money.* When dealing with realtors, always act like you have the money. Once you have a good deal, you can easily get funding from one of your day funders, if you don't have the cash or credit to do the deal yourself. And by this time, you have a database of motivated buyers who will be lined up to buy this house from you in one day.

If you would like to download the complete scripts that we use and edit them any way you want, you can get them at www.realestatedaytrading.com by clicking on the forms link.

MAKE MULTIPLE OFFERS WITH ONE DEPOSIT CHECK

I actually learned this from one of our realtors who was working as a buyer's agent for us. Because we were making many offers with him, he suggested that we let him hold one $1,000 deposit check in escrow for all of the offers we were submitting, and if we had one accepted, then we would be required to send another $1,000 check. This way, the realtor always had an escrow deposit in a trust account for the offers we were submitting.

PROVIDE PROOF OF FUNDS

Sometimes realtors who don't know you will ask for proof of funds before they will accept a contract. There are several ways to do this. You can send them a copy of your bank statement. If you have built up your lines of credit, like I explained in Chapter 7, you'll have the funds to show the realtor. Be sure to write a check from your credit line to your business bank account as a loan to your company. Then give your business bank statement to the realtor. If you would like to get a proof of funds letter from me for your day funding, go to www.realestatedaytrading.com and click on the tab for day funding. You can get a free proof of funds letter for your day funding without any application or credit check. If you are using a private day funder, get a copy of his or her bank statement. If the realtor gives you a problem, you can simply say with confidence, "Funding is no problem." Then move ahead with the deal.

NEGOTIATING ONE-LINERS THAT WORK LIKE A CHARM

Next, I want to give you a few negotiating one-liners that you can use while you are talking to people on the phone. Like an attorney, I like to ask questions I know the answer to. That way I can emphasize the point I am tying to make.

First of all, I like to ask the question, *"Have you had any offers?"* Chances are they have not. If they say, "No," then I say, "Oh." Then I stay silent. The silence punctuates the fact that they are having a hard time selling the house and makes them more motivated.

And if they have had an offer, I ask them, *"Why did you turn it down?"*

I like to ask questions I know the answer to. For example, if I am talking to someone about a two-bedroom, one-bath, wood frame house built in the 50s, I would ask, *"Does it have a pool?"*

They respond, "No." I say, "Oh." I say it like I am disappointed because I expected a pool.

Here is another line that I actually learned from Carlton Sheets, who is a great trainer and investor. I actually bought his course many years ago and learned a lot from it.

"I am looking at another house and although I like yours better, the other one makes more sense." Now they cannot really argue with you about that, can they? But the bottom line is it lets them know that their price is too high.

Here is another good question I like to ask people: *"What will you do if you don't sell?"* I like to get their reaction to that, and I always write down their answers. If their answer is, "I guess I'll rent it out, this may be a good property for seller financing."

An excellent question to ask investors when trying to buy their property is: *"Knowing what you know about this property, would you buy it at this price?"* This is an awesome question to ask, because it makes them reveal any problems with the property or the real reason they are selling.

SECRETS TO SUCCESSFUL NEGOTIATIONS
Adopt a Win-Win Attitude

In negotiations, it is important to adopt a win-win attitude. Some negotiators take a combative stance. But I believe firmly that the best negotiators are cooperative rather than combative. The goal is to reach an accord where the goals of both the buyer and the seller are met. I've seen some buyers try to move sellers to lower their price by pointing out all the deficiencies in the house. This always backfires. Sellers know they have repair problems in their house. They don't need you reminding them. It always backfires and alienates the seller. It is best to base your pricing on the reality of the marketplace. There's no need to make derogatory comments about a person's home.

Sometimes a seller or agent will use combative tactics on you. What do you do? Always respond in an unemotional way. Keep the interchange on a professional level. Don't stoop to arguing. Don't ignore their statements. Just listen intently, and let them know you understand what they are saying. Don't however, let them browbeat you. Just listen, and do not accept or reject. Say you'll think it over and get back to them.

When you do respond, make it clear that your offer is carefully calculated based on the market and the condition of the house. Let them know that the price has not been chosen arbitrarily.

Develop and Maintain Trust

Negotiating the sale of a house is a high-anxiety situation. Sometimes that clouds people's judgment and makes them behave irrationally. People want to be reasonable and fair-minded. But many times sellers are under a lot of pressure to sell the house quickly. Especially motivated sellers. Create a personal relationship of trust with the seller. Be respectful and let them know you are aware of their needs. If you show you are acting with integrity, they will be more cooperative with you. This doesn't mean putting all your cards on the table. It just means treating the person with kindness.

You can show your respect by always listening to what the seller has to say. Respond promptly to counteroffers. Make it clear that you are someone who buys and sells a lot of houses and you have the means to close quickly for all cash. Once you follow the steps outlined to line up your funding, you will be able to say this with confidence.

Listen and understand what the seller has to say. Let sellers know some things about you personally, your hobbies, your favorite sports team or where you went to school.

Use Your Power of Leverage

You have some natural leverage in a situation where you are buying houses from distressed sellers. The leverage in any selling situation depends on what the seller needs. Some are in default and need to move quickly. Others could wait, but are willing to make a move if you offer cash. Find out as much as you can about the seller's needs. Then find solutions for those needs. Offer concessions that solve the seller's problems and address their needs.

Be Patient and Confident

When it comes to negotiations, the tortoise always beats the hare. Be patient. Allow the negotiation process to unfold naturally. Don't worry about the end result, and don't rush headlong to the goal. Just take it a step at a time. And always be confident that you can reach an agreement with the seller. The seller will be looking at you for clues as to whether you can make a deal. You always have to be confident and supportive.

Always Be Willing to Walk Away

Don't fall in love with a deal. One deal is not going to make or break you. Remember this. You lose your power in any negotiation if you want the deal too much. Sellers sense it if you come in with an attitude that you really need the deal. They'll resist you and hold out for the highest possible price. Never give a seller an advantage over you by wanting a deal too much.

Also, be willing to give up a deal where there is no deal. Many beginner investors make this mistake. They have invested a lot of time in calling sellers and making offers, and finally they find one who is interested and wants to negotiate. But after a lot of back and forth, the terms are still not acceptable. The price is above your maximum allowable price. Beginners keep trying to make this no-deal into a deal. Deals like this are not worth it. They waste a lot of time and are discouraging to the beginning investor. Always be willing to walk away.

CHAPTER 11

DUE DILIGENCE: SEPARATING FACT FROM OPINION—VERIFY EVERYTHING THEY TOLD YOU ON THE FIRST PHONE CALL

Now you have a deal. The next step is to perform your due diligence by having your contractor and appraiser inspect and appraise the house. You have 15 days to do this, and about 15 days after that you'll close. If these reports validate the assumptions you made in your instant property analysis, then you close on the deal.

If the inspection and appraisal differ significantly from the assumptions you made, then you want to renegotiate the deal. If you can't renegotiate, then you pass on this deal. This is the safety factor you need when you make offers on houses. You can make bold offers on houses over the phone without even seeing them. You have three clauses in your contract that give you a way out of any deal that's not in your best interest: (1) This contract is subject to a 15-day inspection and approval of the condition of the property prior to closing. (2) This contract is subject to an acceptable appraisal. (3) The deposit shall be the sole remedy in the event of buyer's default.

Only after you get an acceptable inspection and appraisal do you offer the house to your buyers list. Remember, a verified and certified appraisal and inspection make your houses very attractive to buyers/investors. Your buyers know that you have done the due diligence on the house, and they are willing to accept your quick-close terms. Your agreement with buyers only allows them 48 hours to inspect the property after submitting a contract. But if you have already had the house inspected and appraised, those terms are easier for your buyers to accept.

The old way is to let the buyer do the inspection and the appraisal. Just offer the house "as is" to your buyers without any inspection or appraisal. This makes the buyer skeptical, and it takes a long time. The buyer can't close in one day. You only have 30 days to close or you lose the deal and your deposit. Doing things the old way is risky. Your deal might expire before the buyer finishes his inspection and appraisal. And if the appraisal comes in too low, then it's too late to renegotiate with the seller. Your buyer will back out, and you will lose the deal. Getting the inspection and appraisal before you advertise the house to your buyers solves all these problems.

Now that you've signed a contract, time is of the essence. You've got to move fast. The first thing you should do is contact three general contractors from your database and ask them to go out to the property and give you an estimate of repairs.

ORDER THE TITLE SEARCH

After your inspection comes in, call your title company or attorney (depending on what's required in your state), order a title search, and let them know you will have a closing soon and the date. Why wait until closing to find out the status of the title? Now remember, you're not ordering title insurance, just a simple title. It's no big deal, and your title company can do it in a couple of days. If they want to sell title insurance tell them they can talk to your buyer about title insurance. All you want is a title search and to set up a closing.

Your title company will search for every available record or document that relates to present and prior ownership of the property in question with the goal of clearly defining the current status of the property title. In layman's terms, we want to be sure that the property being sold truly and completely belongs to the seller and that he or she has the legal right to transfer ownership of the property.

Your title company will search public and court records, property tax records, deeds, mortgages, wills, judgments, divorce decrees, liens, claims, and other legal proceedings or findings. Any defects found in the title to the property will have to be cleared or otherwise dealt with prior to transferring ownership.

As a real estate day trader, you won't need title insurance, unless for some unforeseen reason you are holding a property for more than a few hours. But even if title has been searched and cleared prior to the sale, your buyer/investor will still need title insurance. Even the most thorough title search may fail to find certain risks, which due to their nature, are "hidden" and not necessarily documented.

If a cloud on the title surfaces at a later date, a title insurance policy will cover your buyer/investor for the costs of a legal defense. If the court upholds the claim, the policy will reimburse your buyer/investor for all or part of the actual loss, depending on the value of the policy. Title insurance is a must for your buyer/investor, but you shouldn't need it when you're day trading real estate.

CONTROL CONTRACTORS TO GET A VALID REPAIR ESTIMATE

At this point, it's time to arrange for the inspection. Remember, we are going to use licensed general contractors who have experience dealing with investors. First, I tell them that I want an estimate of what needs to be done to bring this house into tip-top shape for selling. I want them to give me bids on only those things that are required to get the house back into condition to sell, and no more.

I don't want room additions, upgrades, or enhancements. I'm not trying to make this house better than it was when it was new. I just want things repaired that should have been repaired by the homeowners to keep it in good resale condition. We're not going to break down walls, make a bigger bathroom, add skylights, create a master suite, or add a sunroom. We just want a comfortable livable house that is in good repair.

Then I give each of the contractors an "Investment Property Inspection Report" (Figure 11.1). This is a written and itemized list of things that might need to be done on any property. You can download a copy of this report and make copies in the forms section at www.RealEstateDayTrading.com/Bonuses. It covers:

- *Landscaping:* Patio/deck, pool, driveway
- *Exterior:* Foundation, roofing, wood exterior, siding, porches, garage
- *Interior:* Windows, carpeting, hardwood floors, walls, ceilings, bedrooms, kitchen, bathrooms, dining room, family room, den, attic, basement
- *Systems:* Plumbing, electrical, heating, A/C system, sewer/septic, water
- *Appliances:* Stove, washer, dryer, refrigerator, dishwasher

Date of Inspection _____

Property Address _____
              Street   City   State   Zip

Borrower _____ **Phone** _____

Contractor _____ **Phone** _____

CONDITION	Poor	Average	Good	Excellent	Comments	Estimated Cost of Repairs
1) Landscaping	☐	☐	☐	☐	_____	$ _____
A. Patio/Deck	☐	☐	☐	☐	_____	$ _____
B. Pool	☐	☐	☐	☐	_____	$ _____
C. Driveway	☐	☐	☐	☐	_____	$ _____
D. _____ (Other)	☐	☐	☐	☐	_____	$ _____
2) Exterior						
A. Foundation	☐	☐	☐	☐	_____	$ _____
B. Roofing	☐	☐	☐	☐	_____	$ _____
C. Wood Exterior	☐	☐	☐	☐	_____	$ _____
D. Siding	☐	☐	☐	☐	_____	$ _____
E. Porches	☐	☐	☐	☐	_____	$ _____
F. Garage	☐	☐	☐	☐	_____	$ _____
G. _____ (Other)	☐	☐	☐	☐	_____	$ _____
H. _____ (Other)	☐	☐	☐	☐	_____	$ _____
3) Interior						
A. Windows	☐	☐	☐	☐	_____	$ _____
B. Carpeting	☐	☐	☐	☐	_____	$ _____
C. Hdwd. Floors	☐	☐	☐	☐	_____	$ _____
D. Walls/Ceilings	☐	☐	☐	☐	_____	$ _____
E. Bedroom #1	☐	☐	☐	☐	_____	$ _____
Bedroom #2	☐	☐	☐	☐	_____	$ _____
Bedroom #3	☐	☐	☐	☐	_____	$ _____
Bedroom #4	☐	☐	☐	☐	_____	$ _____
F. Kitchen	☐	☐	☐	☐	_____	$ _____
G. Bathroom #1	☐	☐	☐	☐	_____	$ _____
Bathroom #2	☐	☐	☐	☐	_____	$ _____
Bathroom #3	☐	☐	☐	☐	_____	$ _____
H. Dining Room	☐	☐	☐	☐	_____	$ _____
I. Family Room	☐	☐	☐	☐	_____	$ _____
J. Den	☐	☐	☐	☐	_____	$ _____
K. Attic	☐	☐	☐	☐	_____	$ _____
L. Basement	☐	☐	☐	☐	_____	$ _____
M. _____ (Other)	☐	☐	☐	☐	_____	$ _____

FIGURE 11.1   Investment Property Inspection Report

CONDITION	Poor	Average	Good	Excellent	Comments	Estimated Cost of Repairs
4) Systems						
A. Plumbing	☐	☐	☐	☐	_____	$ _____
B. Electrical	☐	☐	☐	☐	_____	$ _____
C. Heating	☐	☐	☐	☐	_____	$ _____
D. A/C System	☐	☐	☐	☐	_____	$ _____
E. Sewer/Septic	☐	☐	☐	☐	_____	$ _____
F. Water	☐	☐	☐	☐	_____	$ _____
G. _____ (Other)	☐	☐	☐	☐	_____	$ _____
5) Appliances						
A. Stove	☐	☐	☐	☐	_____	$ _____
B. Washer	☐	☐	☐	☐	_____	$ _____
C. Dryer	☐	☐	☐	☐	_____	$ _____
D. Refrigerator	☐	☐	☐	☐	_____	$ _____
E. Dishwasher	☐	☐	☐	☐	_____	$ _____
F. _____ (Other)	☐	☐	☐	☐	_____	$ _____

Total Estimated Cost of Repairs $ _____

☐ Does the property have any Code Violations
   Initials _____

☐ Attach Photo of House

☐ List of Code Violations Is Attached
   Initials _____

☐ House Is Secure

Can we increase the # of bedrooms or add a bathroom within the existing sq. footage?
_____Cost $ _____

Condition of Surrounding Houses: (circle one)   Well Maintained   Decent   Poor   Distressed

Any Vacancies on Street: (circle one)   None Apparent   Few   Many

If so what are the addresses? _____

I certify that the above listed repairs will be performed in a safe, sound, and sanitary manner and will justify the estimated repair costs listed above.

By: _____   Date: _____
                        (Contractor)

Borrower: _____   Date: _____

FIGURE 11.1   (*Continued*)

The report lists the condition of each of these items and provides an estimate of item-by-item repair costs, as well as the total estimated cost of repairs. I also ask my contractors to attach a photo of the house. And I ask the questions in Figure 11.1.

With my "Investment Property Inspection Report," each of the three contactors must estimate repairs based on the same specifications. If one of them thinks the bathroom tile needs to be replaced and the other two don't, then I'll know that that contractor is padding the estimate with unnecessary work. This form keeps my contractors honest. You can also look at each item to see how each contractor bid. If one contractor comes in with higher costs on each item, I'll know that he is bidding too high. This document puts me in control. And the contractors give me a report on vacant houses in the area while they are there. This is valuable bonus information that is helpful to me.

Another trick I learned from my good friend Pete Youngs, also known as Mr. Rehab: When getting bids on a property, get three bids and take the lowest one, then get three more bids and show the lowest bid from the first three bids to the second three contractors as a guide. This way they will all try to beat that price. You can learn a lot about rehabbing houses at www.PeteYoungs.com.

Treat Good Contractors Like Gold

My contractors are my eyes; they are looking at my properties for me. They have to give me their honest opinion and let me know what I need to know to make an informed decision. When I find a good one I treat that contractor like gold.

You want to build a relationship with a rehab contractor. You're having them give you free estimates on your properties, and you have to remember to give them something in return. If you buy the properties and your buyer/investor uses them for the repairs, they'll make out on the deal.

But, if you have a contractor go out to over five properties to write up estimates, but you do not end up buying any of them, you need to start paying them to do the next few estimates until you actually buy one of the properties and they actually get the job. Remember to create win-win situations and don't wait until the contractor has to tell you that they can't give you any more free estimates because they haven't gotten any jobs out of it yet. Just start paying them after they've done five estimates for you without getting any work. You don't have to pay them much, maybe

$100 to $200. But once they actually get a job going with you, then you can stop paying for the estimates again.

USE HOME INSPECTORS FOR PROPERTIES THAT NEED A LOT OF WORK

If the property needs a lot of work, you should have a licensed home inspector look at it as well. The reason we do not do this on every job is because the home inspector will charge you for a report. It usually costs around $300 to $400, and it will not even include an estimate of repair costs. But when you're dealing with problem houses, there may be some hidden problems that your contractors don't find. If these problems exist, you need to know about them before you buy the house because then you can go back to your seller and negotiate a much lower price.

If you are going to get a licensed home inspector to inspect the property, he'll do it after you receive your estimate from the contractor. Make sure that the rehab estimate is within budget before paying for a home inspection. Sometimes the home inspection will turn up some problems not addressed by your contractors. If this happens, ask your contractors to quote the additional repairs that need to be done.

FIND OUT THE REAL DEAL ON THE NEIGHBORHOOD

Before buying, you want to discover as much as you can about the neighborhood. As I said earlier, you want to buy houses in low- to medium-income neighborhoods. You don't want to buy in high crime areas or war zones. Sometimes you can't tell by looking at it that an area is a war zone. To get the real deal on a neighborhood, call the local police department on a nonemergency line. When you get someone on the phone ask, "Is this a nonemergency line?" If they say yes, then ask them if you can get a police report for all of the activity in the neighborhood where your property is located. Some will have a web site where you can get the information, and some will have to mail it to you.

You should also contact the local building inspection or code enforcement department to make sure that there are no code violations on the subject property. If there are, you need to get a list. This is also a good time to ask them for a list of all of the properties under code enforcement so that you can try to buy these properties also.

CANCEL A CONTRACT AND/OR NEGOTIATE A BETTER DEAL

Once you get the contractors estimate, if the costs are the same as you had estimated, then you can get an appraisal to see if the appraisal comes in on target.

If the repair costs are above your original estimate, do another instant property analysis using the repair costs your contractor gave you. Calculate a new maximum allowable price. If the price in your contract with the seller is above the new maximum allowable price, then consider renegotiating the deal.

After you get your rehab estimate or home inspection report, it's a great time to go back to the seller to renegotiate a better price, especially if the report came in with more repairs than you anticipated. Please do not take advantage of anyone, but use it as a great negotiating tool when you need to.

Figure 11.2 is a letter that you can send to the realtor or seller when you need to back out of a contract because the inspection report or repair estimate came in too high. Remember, you can't make any money if you don't buy any property. So the purpose of the letter is not to back out of the deal but to renegotiate a better deal. You can also use this same letter if the appraisal comes in too low. Substitute the repair sentence with a sentence saying the appraisal came in too low.

After sending the letter, contact the owner/seller or the realtor to tell them about the letter you've sent and to find out if they would be willing to renegotiate another contract based on the new information that just surfaced. Then start the negotiation process and try to work out a deal that would benefit both parties. Be gentle, be conciliatory, and keep the dialogue rational.

By having the letter in writing, if you can't renegotiate a better deal, then you have the right to get your deposit back based on the terms of the contract. But don't cancel a contract often. Do it only when necessary or you'll get the reputation of being a flake and realtors won't want to deal with you.

If you can't renegotiate a deal that suits you, you might want to cancel the deal. But before you cancel, think about all the issues. Consider how much you are paying above the maximum price. If you agreed to pay $36,965, and the new maximum allowable price is $38,543, then your fee will be reduced by $1,578. In this case, you may want to go ahead with the deal anyway depending on how much profit you had in the deal.

<Date>

Realtor Agency *(If buying from realtor)*
Realtor or Seller's Name
Address
City, State, Zip

Your Company name *(if using one)*
Your Name
Address
City, State, Zip

Re: Property Address/MLS Number (if applicable)

Dear <*Name*>,

After inspection of the above referenced property, I (*we*) have determined that more repairs than initially anticipated are needed. Due to the associated costs of the additional repairs, I (*we*) are exercising (*my/our*) option to cancel the contract on said property within the inspection period.

If you have received an escrow check, please refund the deposit at your earliest convenience to the address below.

If you have any questions, please do not hesitate to give me a call.

Sincerely,

<*Your Name*>

<*Your Contact Info*>

Copyright © 2009 by Larry Goins. To customize this document, download Figure 11.2 to your hard drive from www.realestatedaytrading.com/bonuses. The document can then be opened, edited, and printed using Microsoft Word or another popular word processing application.

FIGURE 11.2   Cancel Contract Letter to Realtor

Another thing to consider is your reputation. Let's say this is your first deal and after the repair estimate comes in, your fee is reduced by $3,442. You might think, "Why should I bother?" But you've done most of the work, you won't get your full fee, but you'll get something out of it. And your realtor will make a commission on the deal, and you'll be a hero in his or her eyes. You'll get a house for your credibility kit, and the word will spread that you are the real McCoy. In this case, it's still worth it to go through with the deal.

I did a deal just like this a while back where I only made $1,500 and closed on it just to keep the realtor happy. I told the realtor that I would normally back out because of the higher repair estimate, but I wanted to build a long-term business relationship with him, so I was going to close instead. The realtor understood and appreciated me telling him and closing on the deal. I have done several deals with this realtor since. Remember that I didn't include closing costs in these figures.

Obviously if you stand to lose money, and the seller refuses to renegotiate, you'll definitely want to cancel, get your deposit back, and move on to another deal with more room to make money.

VALIDATE APPRAISALS TO FIND OUT WHAT THE PROPERTY IS REALLY WORTH

As soon as we know how much it will cost to get the home repaired, then we must find out what it will be worth after the repairs are made, if any are needed. We will be getting an appraisal based on the *after-repaired* value or *subject to* the improvements.

I know there are free online services to give you comparisons and those are great for your preliminary due diligence. Here are several you can use: reply.com, housevalues.com, ditech.com, instanthomevaluations.com, electronicappraiser.com, and Free-Home-Appraisal.com. Use these for a quick estimate of a home's value. You can even look up the value while still on the phone with the seller or realtor to save time and make a more accurate offer on the first phone call.

But remember, they are not completely reliable. Lenders will not accept these quick online appraisals. You cannot use them in place of an appraisal by a licensed appraiser. Before you buy a property, you want to know the true value based on a true appraisal by a licensed appraiser.

An appraisal is a standard property valuation report used by lending institutions. It is thought to be a highly accurate estimate of value from a local, licensed appraiser. The appraiser will visit the house and supply you with a written report that will include an estimated market value based on comparisons with other houses within one mile of your house that have sold recently. The closer the comparison houses are in size and type, in proximity, and recency of sale, the better the appraisal. Standard appraisal reports include comparable sales, formulas, and the qualifications of the appraiser.

When looking for appraisers, you want to find one who is familiar with investment property. You also want one who is fairly conservative. You don't need an appraiser fluffing up the value of your property. If you buy it on a bad appraisal, it does you no good. You might get stuck with the property when your buyer's lender orders its own appraisal, and it comes in much lower than yours. Then you are stuck with a house for which you overpaid.

Give the appraiser the property inspection report you got from your rehab contractor. Tell the appraiser to give you the after-repair value. Appraisers are very familiar with this and will have no trouble providing it. And remember, your house is not complex. It's not a big luxury house with lots of complex appliances, add-ons, upgrades, and expensive enhancements that may or may not really improve the market value of the home. Your appraiser is dealing with a bread-and-butter house that is much like the other houses in the neighborhood.

While appraisals on big expensive homes can vary drastically, these simple, three-bedroom, two-bath houses were punched out by the dozens, and one is pretty much the same as the other. We call them *cookie-cutter houses*. The appraisal for one is going to be similar to another. As long as the house is repaired and in good condition, it will sell for about the same price as other similar houses in the area. In dealing with these houses, there are very seldom any surprises. These houses are easy to appraise for most appraisers, and they should be able to complete the appraisal for you promptly.

READ/EVALUATE AN APPRAISAL REPORT IN THREE SECONDS FLAT

I want to share a quick and easy method to use when looking at an appraisal to help you determine whether your lender or underwriter will have a problem with the appraisal. I learned this from an appraisal class.

When you get an appraisal on a property you are trying to buy, look at all the pictures in it. Look at the subject property and all of the comparable sales or comps. Then, choose the house you would *least* like to live in. If there is a noticeable difference, and it is *your* house that looks the worst, then the underwriter will definitely have a problem with the appraisal.

Lenders are looking for good comps with the fewest number of adjustments. For example, sometimes if an appraiser cannot find a good comp close to your property, he will go miles away to find a similar house. But that house might be located in a better neighborhood than yours. So the appraiser has to make an adjustment in price. Sometimes the comp matches in size and is located in the same neighborhood, but it is newer. It looks nicer and has curb appeal.

That house will sell for a much higher price than yours. The appraiser will adjust the price of your house downward to accommodate the difference in the comp. This is a perfectly normal and ethical way of coming up with an appraised value. So your appraiser is not doing anything wrong. It's just not a method that will be to your benefit.

The pictures of the other houses will look nicer than your house. And this will make the lender suspicious. It is just human nature. We really do judge a book by its cover. A better-looking house always fetches a higher price. If your house is being compared to better-looking houses, the lender will probably reject it. So always check to see which house looks the worst. If it is your house, then you've got a problem. You need a better appraisal. Tell the appraiser to find comps of houses that are closer to your house in age and value. Don't let him compare superstar houses to your ordinary-Joe house.

Remember, this is just a quick method and is by no means a definite way to tell if you have a good appraisal. There are many things that underwriters look for, such as the gross and net adjustments. Don't worry if you do not understand all of the details about appraisals. As you become more familiar with the whole process it will come together for you.

CHAPTER 12

ONLINE BIDDING WARS: CREATE AN INSIDER LIST OF PREQUALIFIED, SUPERMOTIVATED BUYERS WHO CAN AND WILL BUY YOUR HOUSES IN TWO HOURS OR LESS

Now that we have done our due diligence and know the exact dollar amount on repairs and what the property will sell for, it is time to sell it fast! The next step is to advertise the house to your buyers list.

TURN UP THE HEAT AND CREATE A BUYING FRENZY

In this business, you will come to realize that Pareto's law works in real estate day trading just as it does in so many other businesses. The Pareto principle, also known as the 80/20 rule, states that, for many events, 80 percent of the effects come from 20 percent of the causes. It is a common rule of thumb in business that 80 percent of your sales come from 20 percent of your clients.

I've found this to be true in real estate day trading. About 20 percent of my buyers account for about 80 percent of my sales. Once I noticed it, I decided to capitalize on it. I asked, "Why should I spend my time with the 80 percent, when the 20 percent are giving me most of my sales?"

Then I wondered, "How can I get more involved with the 20 percent who do most of the buying." That's when I found out about the *whisper campaign*.

THE SECRET OF THE WHISPER CAMPAIGN

The whisper campaign is a term and a process that I learned from a real estates salesperson who worked for a company that sold waterfront property. And they sell a lot of it! They create a buying frenzy by using the principle of urgency. People generally procrastinate. Many people wait until the last moment to do anything. Then they get motivated. Anything can cause this: an impending price increase, running out of product, or lots of other people bidding on the same property. In this case, the real estate salesperson created a scenario in which the properties seemed to be scarce.

Limited supply was the motivating factor. The salesperson made it known to everyone that everyone else was buying these properties. The salesperson's line, "Supply is scarce and once we run out of properties, you might be left out." Nobody wants to be left out. Remember, these people are interested in these properties and have been considering buying them. But they have been putting off the decision, as many people do. Now the time has come for them to take action. It is a great sales tool.

In real estate day trading, we need to do the same thing. Again we have buyers who are interested in the properties. They have the means and inclination to make a purchase. Now we use two things to create a buying frenzy: scarcity of time and scarcity of access.

SCARCITY OF TIME

First you must create a scarcity of time. This is easy to do, and it is believable because it is true. You really are short on time. You've got to sell fast because you only have 30 days before the contract expires. When you advertise your first deal, be sure to mention that the deals go fast and you accept contracts on a first-come–first-served basis. Then stick with it. This is the beauty of having a database filled with motivated buyers. You can contact them all at one time and have them fight to be the first one to get the contract to you. It's sort of like an auction. In auctions, the heat of competition stimulates people's combative nature. The need to win at all costs sometimes ends up costing people a lot more than if they bought in a slow deliberate process.

Houses sold at auction always pull more sales at higher prices than houses that are listed.

Keep track of how long your property took to sell (e.g., two hours). Now in this kind of selling environment, a lot of people who made bids lost out. Many other people were thinking of bidding but waited too long, and the house ended up being sold before some could even make an offer. This is good. Your buyers are learning (1) your houses are selling fast, and (2) you were telling them the truth when you said the house would go fast.

After the house is sold, be sure to send an e-mail telling your buyers that the house sold in just two hours (or however many hours it actually took). Even if it took three days, you want to say 72 hours because hours sound better than days. Then everyone will become aware of how fast they have to respond in order to get a contract accepted. This will set the stage for an even greater frenzy, the next time you have a house for sale.

Figure 12.1 is a sample script you can use in an e-mail.

Dear <first name>,

I just wanted to send out a short e-mail to let you know that the property at _____ _____ St. sold in a record _____ hours. It was a great deal for the buyer and should be closing soon.

Please stop e-mailing and calling about this one because we have been overwhelmed answering all of the calls and responding to all of the e-mails.

As you can see, our properties go very fast. We will send out an e-mail with all of the information about the next property we get.

In order to get one of our properties, you have to act fast. We really appreciate your business and look forward to working with you.

Thank You,

<Your Name>

FIGURE 12.1   Whisper Campaign E-Mail

SCARCITY OF ACCESS: CREATE A TWO-HOUR HEAD START SHORT LIST

The next task in managing your whisper campaign is to create a short list that gets only the best-qualified buyers looking at your properties. The whole idea behind it is to get the word out about your newly available properties to a few select, qualified people (before everyone else) to get the properties sold fast. This is your *short list*.

This creates an amazing buying frenzy because everyone then wants to be a part of the short list in order to get advanced notification of deals. This is an example of creating a sense of urgency by using scarcity of access.

Create an upper echelon of special buyers who get to know about your deals first. Send an e-mail to each buyer in your entire database letting them know that you are creating a short list of buyers to contact first with the next property you have available. You will get a lot of people who want to be included.

MAKE SURE THEY ARE QUALIFIED BEFORE YOU CLICK SEND

Another reason I came up with the short list is to make the selling process more efficient. Most investors who get into the business already have a full-time job. If you have a property to sell and you have 100 investors on your buyers list, you can send out 100 e-mails, but then you will be answering 20 to 30 e-mails and calling back 10 to 20 people when you only need one buyer. That's not a good use of your time.

I came up with the idea of the *two-hour head start short list*, to prevent you from wasting your time with unqualified buyers. Think about it. The realtors make sure a prospect is qualified before they will drive a client around in a car. Why should we be any different from the realtors? The only difference with my short list is that we don't have to drive them around and buy them lunch. We are going to make sure they are qualified before we even click send.

HARD MONEY LENDERS PREQUALIFY YOUR BUYERS FOR YOU

Make sure to prequalify your buyers. You want to make sure they have the money and credit to be able to buy property with all cash in a short time frame. It's easy to do this. Just align yourself with hard money lenders who understand investor lending. They will prequalify your buyers for you. Most hard money lenders will prequalify buyers by checking their credit scores and making sure they have enough extra funding on hand in case of emergencies like going over budget or running into unanticipated problems. Hard money lenders can fund both the property acquisition and the repairs.

They offer great benefit to buyers—no money down, quick closings, and financing based on appraisal, sometimes in excess of the appraised value. Banks never do this. The typical hard money loan is for a maximum of one year. Usually hard money lenders protect themselves by releasing cash as work is completed.

One year is plenty of time for the buyer/investor to get the repairs completed and the property refinanced or sold. If your buyers are prequalified with a hard money lender, they can close fast on your deals. Make sure anyone you allow on your short list (Figure 12.2) has prequalified with a hard money lender or can pay cash.

In the future, send notices of any houses you have for sale to this list first and watch the offers come in! Then send an e-mail to your entire database to let everyone know that the property is sold already. This is like an auction, only better! You will soon start getting e-mails from buyers wanting you to call them first with the next property.

The most important thing I can say here is to never, never lie about a property: the value, the price, how long it took to sell, or anything else. It is extremely important that all properties presented and sent out in the e-mail are actual deals. You want to create the image of having real deals that are good investments and that sell fast. Once you build a reputation for offering these kinds of deals, then you will have people fighting to buy your houses.

SECURE BACKUP CONTRACTS

The best policy for you is to get backup contracts on each deal in case a buyer drops out at the last moment. If you create a buying frenzy as I've explained, you will be able to accept a primary buying contract and put a couple more on hold as backups in case you need another buyer.

That's how I've been able to day trade so many houses throughout my career. Using this system, selling in two hours is no problem. Using this system, we've been able to have a ready buyer waiting to close on every house we've bought, with backup buyers standing by. With this system, you can't lose!

Dear Larry,

In order to better serve my investors, we are offering a "Two-Hour, First-To-Know" short list opportunity to get a first look at all of our properties.

To remain on the short list please read this e-mail very carefully.

My overall e-mail list consists of over 3,500 people, and every time I market a new property it is sent to several places, including my e-mail lists and several Yahoo News Groups. Over 5,000 people have an opportunity to view the property; however, I have a growing list of investors (64 people) that always get first pick.

This is a small group of serious, prequalified investors, capable of making fast decisions and closing very quickly. These investors only need 24 hours to inspect the property, then we close.

In order to maintain the integrity of this group and be placed on our short list, please send the following information to us as soon as possible.

- Are you prequalified, if so, who is it with?
- Do you have a prequalification letter or a copy of a bank statement?
- Can you write an earnest money check and overnight it?
- Can you close fast?
- What type of property are you looking for?
- What area are you investing in?
- How long have you been investing?
- What are your investment goals?

By providing us with this information, you will be able to get a two-hour head start over everyone else on our list of investors. We are only allowing 10 investors to be on this list, so please send us your information as soon as possible to insure that you are able to get on this list.

You don't have to be prequalified through our company, but I need to know that you are ready to buy. The easiest thing to do is go to our website, www.financialhelpservices.com and click "apply online." Fill in your financial information. (Use the address 1234 Anywhere St, Anytown, USA)

That's it. I realize this may seem a little personal, but I want to know my investors.

Thanks for your help, and I hope your investing is going well. If there is anything I can do, please let me know. Our company also provides investor education, so if you have questions, please give me a call or e-mail.

Thank you,

Larry Goins
Larry@LarryGoins.com
FINANCIAL HELP SERVICES, INC.
WWW.FINANCIALHELPSERVICES.COM
4543 Charlotte Hwy - Suite 15
Lake Wylie, SC 29710
Office: 803.831.0056 (Ext 304)
Fax: 803.831.0805
HARD MONEY LOANS & 100% FINANCING & INVESTOR EDUCATION & TRAINING

Copyright © 2009 by Larry Goins. To customize this document, download Figure 12.2 to your hard drive from www.realestatedaytrading.com/bonuses. The document can then be opened, edited, and printed using Microsoft Word or another popular word processing application.

FIGURE 12.2   Short List E-mail Sample

GET CONTRACT EXTENSIONS
FROM YOUR SELLER

I've talked a lot about buying and selling in a 30-day time limit. But what happens if time runs out and you can't find a buyer before the 30-day time limit. In reality, it's not the end of the world. It happens that sometimes you don't get all the details ironed out in 30 days. If your contract runs out, it is not the end. Most of the time, you can negotiate with a motivated seller to give you more time. If you are near closing and need a few more days, most owners/sellers, banks, and realtors will want the deal to go through as much as you do and will often give you more time.

CHAPTER 13

Let's Get Paid: Bought at 10:00 am, Sold at 10:30 am

Finally it's payday, and all your hard work is about to pay off. You are about to collect your $5,000 or more paycheck. The whole procedure takes place in just 30 minutes. If you close on buying a house at 10:00 AM, you can turn around and close on selling it by 10:30 AM. And you'll walk away with your $5,000 plus check. Now this is where the excellent dream team of professionals will serve you well.

Once you have a contract from a buyer/investor, your inspection and appraisal are complete, and everything looks good, then immediately contact your attorney or title company to prepare all the documents for the close. Your attorney or title company is your representative at the closing and will handle everything for you. It's their job to make sure that all the complex details of a real estate closing are carried out swiftly and efficiently.

You don't even need to be there, if you don't want to be. I have bought and sold houses all over the country without being present at closing. As a beginner, it would be a good idea for you to attend the closings. But once you get more experience doing deals, you can leave those details to your attorney and title company.

The buyer's/investor's lender (usually a hard money lender, if a lender is involved) deposits the funds needed for closing in the title company's escrow account. You can deposit your funds for purchasing the property with the attorney or title company as well.

If your day funder is providing the funds for you, then your attorney or title company will have the day funder deposit funds in the escrow account. As I explained in Chapter 7, a day funder is a private investor who lends you the money for 24 hours to acquire the property from the seller and immediately sell the house to a buyer/investor that same day. The day funder gets all his or her money back plus a fee when the deal closes.

The first part of the closing is when you buy the house from the seller. Your attorney or title company will take funds from your escrow account and provide a check to the seller. That's the buying half of the day trade. And it shouldn't take more than 15 minutes.

Then, you immediately sell the house to your buyer/investor. This takes another 15 minutes. Your attorney or title company takes funds from your buyer's/investor's escrow account and cuts a check to you. You will usually receive your actual check the next day after all of the proper documents have been filed and recorded. Sometimes it won't all go to you. If you used a day funder to buy the house for you, then the day funder will receive a check for the amount they provided plus their fee, and you will get your $5,000 or more paycheck.

At the same time, the attorney or title company will make sure that all the closing costs are paid to the various parties involved: taxes, title, insurance, attorney fees, points to the lender, and so on, according to the closing statement. After closing, the title company will file the legal documents, and make sure all outstanding liens have been paid.

This is the general scenario if you are paying all cash for the house at closing or using the cash of your day funder to close. Often this is the easiest and fastest way to get the deal done especially when you are dealing with realtors and bankers, who are reluctant to do anything that is outside the ordinary.

CREATIVE WAYS TO CLOSE YOUR DEALS WITHOUT MONEY

There are many ways to close a deal. If you have the cash or a day funder, often the easiest way is to simply use your own or your day funder's cash to close the deal, as I described previously. But don't let the lack of cash stop you from making a good deal. In day trading, funding is not a problem, as long as you have a good deal. If you have used my instant property analysis to run the numbers and found a seller who will sell to you below your maximum allowable price, and a buyer/investor who can buy the property at a price that is at least $5,000 or more higher, then you have everything you need. Now you just need the expertise to arrange the close in a way that doesn't require you to put up any money.

I am going to share some creative ways to close deals in the order of the easiest to the most difficult. You will probably not use all of these, but it is good to know about all of them so you will have more tools in your toolbox and not miss a deal when it comes along.

Assignment of Contract

The first and easiest way is to do an assignment. You will not be able to do an assignment on every deal. Some sellers, especially banks or lenders and most realtors, will not allow you to put an assignment clause in the contract. But when you're dealing directly with a homeowner or investor who is selling property without a realtor, then you can often get an assignment. The added benefit of this method is that you do not have to pay two sets of closing costs or come up with financing for the property.

An assignment is when you do not buy and sell the property, instead you simply assign your existing contract to another person who is stepping into your shoes to complete the contract. Whatever terms you negotiated with the seller are in force for the person you assign to the contract.

Let's say you sign a contract with the seller to buy her house for $32,687 in your name and/or assigns. You can do this by having your seller sign a standard Purchase and Sale Agreement with the buyer listed as "your name AND/OR ASSIGNS." Then you assign the contract to your buyer/investor using an assignment form. Your assignee agrees to pay you an assignment fee of $5,000 or more and buy the property directly from the seller, putting his or her name on the closing documents instead of yours. In this situation there is only one closing. You never buy the house. But you get an assignment fee paid to you out of the buyer's escrow account at closing.

When you assign a contract to your buyer/investor you have that person sign an Assignment of Contract/Interest agreement with you. This contains a clause that states the amount of the assignment fee that will be paid to you at closing. Once your buyer/investor agrees, then you have a right to be paid a fee at closing. Figure 13.1 shows an assignment so that you can have an idea of what it looks like. If you would like to download a fully editable one, you can find it for free at www.RealEstateDayTrading.com/Bonuses.

Assignment of Beneficial Interest

Most of the time when dealing with realtors, they will not allow assignments. They don't want to tie the property up with someone who is going to assign the contract to someone else. Here is a way you can do an assignment even

_____ (Assignor) hereby assigns, transfers, sells the Contract/Interest, whether written or verbal in the property located at _____ _____ in the City of _____, State of _____to _____ _____ (Assignee). The assignment fee of $_____ is to be paid from proceeds at closing. _____ (Assignor) has negotiated a purchase price on the above referenced property of $ _____ which is an "as is/where is" price with no warranties or guarantees. Adding the assignment fee of $ _____, the assignees total purchase price is $ _____ plus any inspection fees, repairs, due diligence, and/or closing costs. In addition to the assignment fee, the assignee shall reimburse assignor the deposit the amount of $_____ _____, which has already been paid by assignor. This assignment is made with no warranties, guarantees, or claims as to condition of property, size, title, or present or future value of property, and it is the assignees' responsibility to perform their own due diligence before closing. This assignment shall survive the closing.

The undersigned agrees that they have the full authority to execute this document personally and for any organization they represent or will represent. By signing, you agree that you have read, understand, and have the full power and authority to enter into this legal agreement. If you do not understand this document, please seek legal counsel prior to signing. The under-signed acknowledges receipt of a copy of this document.

_____   _____   _____
Witness   Assignor   Date

_____   _____   _____
Witness   Assignor   Date

_____   _____   _____
Witness   Assignor   Date

FIGURE 13.1   Assignment of Contract/Interest

though the realtor is only accepting standard nonassignable contracts. This is a way to assign a nonassignable contract.

You can simply create (or have your attorney create) a land trust with you as the beneficiary, then you assign the beneficial interest in the trust to your buyer. When you sign the contract with the seller, use the name of the land trust. It doesn't matter what you name your trust. I would suggest naming the trust the same as the address of the property. Like "125 Falls St. Trust." You create the land trust by signing a trust agreement. Do this before signing the contract to buy the property. You are listed as the beneficiary of the trust. The trust that you create is the entity that actually holds the title of the real estate for you.

At closing, you transfer the beneficial interest in the trust to your buyer/investor. Then your buyer/investor closes with the seller using the name of the trust that you wrote on the contract. Since they are now the beneficiary of the trust, they enjoy full ownership rights of the property. The sale of the house is recorded in the name of the trust. The actual owner of the trust is part of the land trust documentation. It is never publicly recorded.

So when you transfer the ownership of the trust (the beneficial interest), it is a private matter between you and the buyer. When using this technique there is no assignment. You just sell the beneficial interest for the exact same amount you want to make on the deal. My buyer now owns the beneficial interest in the trust that has the property under contract and will buy the property from the seller with whom I negotiated the deal. In the example we've been using throughout this book, that amount is $5,000. Of course this can be set higher if the profit margin in the particular deal warrants it.

Subject To

Subject to is when you buy a property with the existing financing in place and basically continue making payments on the seller's mortgage. This is especially applicable to homeowners in default. I am not a big fan of this method and rarely use it.

But let's be realistic. You can do this by talking the seller into deeding the property to you by promising that you will continue to make payments for them. It works especially well when the homeowner's equity in the property is virtually nonexistent. By taking over the loan, you are helping the homeowner by making the payments for them until you sell the house. The discount you can take is limited by the amount of the loan. If the loan amount it close to the after-repair value, you cannot buy at a discount.

This is not a real estate day trading strategy. You as a real estate day trader are looking for houses in need of repair that you can buy at deep discounts. If you find a house in need of repair, where the bank loan is below the maximum allowable price, then you can get a contract to buy it outright. You can find a buyer and sell it in one day. In this case, you don't need to bother with *subject to*.

There is however a law called the Garn Saint Germain Act, which states that a lender cannot enforce a due-on-sale clause if a property is transferred for estate planning purposes. That is one reason that some investors use the land trust because it is typically an estate planning entity. But in my opinion, using a land trust to get around a due-on-sale clause is not a very ethical way to do business, and I personally don't recommend it.

I know there are many trainers teaching how to do it, and that's fine if it is what you want to do. But personally, I think there are better, more ethical and honest ways to do business than going the slick route.

If the existing loan is higher than the amount of your maximum allowable price after you account for repairs and the after-repaired value, then you can't make any money buying the house anyway. The price you would have to get would be below the amount of the loan. The lender wouldn't agree to this deal. However, you could try to get the lender to agree to a short sale, just to get it off the books.

But remember, you are looking for houses that need repairs that you can buy at a steep discount and resell to buyers/investors at below 70 percent of the after-repair value. That's why buyers are lined up to buy from you. If you step out of this business model and start acquiring houses that don't need repairs and that are only slightly below market value, you could quickly get stuck with houses you can't sell. And that could be costly. Don't stray from the day trading model I've taught you.

Buying subject to is too risky; it could easily backfire on you. I have seen many new investors who focused on getting a deed and then couldn't sell the property because they couldn't acquire the property at a low enough price to sell it to a buyer/investor. At that point, they have to go back and return it to the seller. This causes a lot of complaints, which could cost you a lot of money or even land you in court.

That's why many states have enacted laws to protect consumers against investors who buy a property subject to. Another risk is that the lender will call the loan because the borrower has violated the bank's due-on-sale clause by deeding the property to you subject to. I have never seen a bank do this because as long as they receive their payments, they are usually happy. If you are going to buy a property with this method, make sure that you can afford to make the payments no matter what. After all, you told the seller that you would.

Options

Options are another way to close a transaction. In an option, you really do not have a contract on the property but an option to buy the property at a certain price and for a certain length of time. The money you give the seller as option money is nonrefundable because it is the price you are paying for the option itself. You can then decide if you want to exercise the option or not.

If you find a buyer before the option period ends, you exercise the option and close on the property. If you do not find a buyer for your option before the option expires, then you only lose your option money, no more. In this type of transaction, you also will not need any more cash than the price of the option. Only pay a nominal amount to the seller for the option ($10 or $50); although, I have paid several hundred dollars for options if it was a really good deal and it was the only way I could get the seller to give me an option.

Most realtors do not want to submit options because they want an actual contract on the property and do not want to have to take the property off of the market during the option period. And their clients don't want them to do that, either. It's rare that a realtor will accept an option contract on anything but houses in the most dire circumstances.

The best types of properties for sellers to use an option with are houses that are for sale by owner or by involuntary owners. They also work well on luxury homes if the seller is having trouble selling it. Look for owners who are stuck with a house they can't sell, that needs repairs, and who are financially strapped. In this situation, you might be their only hope for selling the house.

Here are some types of sellers who might be willing to accept an option contract because it's better than nothing: divorce, delinquent property taxes, out-of-town owners, vacant houses, houses listed with code enforcement, homeowners in transition, bail bonding companies, surplus property owned by the city, nonprofit organizations, mobile home dealers, private money lenders, hard money lenders, tired landlords, and damaged houses. Chapter 6 explains how to find these desperate buyers.

I have included two option agreements for you. The first one (Figure 13.2) is a standard option agreement, "Option Agreement for Purchase of Real Property." The second one (Figure 13.3) is what we call a

THIS OPTION AGREEMENT ("Agreement") made and entered into this _____ day of _____, 200___, by and between _____, whose principal address is _____, hereinafter referred to as "Seller" and _____, whose principal address is _____, hereinafter referred to as "Purchaser":

WITNESSETH:

WHEREAS, Seller is the fee simple owner of certain real property being, lying, and situated in the County of _____, State of _____, such real property having the street address of _____ ("Premises") and such property being more particularly described as follows:
(legal description here)

Also known as

_____

WHEREAS, Purchaser desires to procure an option to purchase the Premises upon the terms and provisions as hereinafter set forth;

NOW, THEREFORE, for good and valuable consideration the receipt and sufficiency of which is hereby acknowledged by the parties hereto and for the mutual covenants contained herein, Seller and Purchaser hereby agree as follows:

1. **DEFINITIONS.** For the purposes of this Agreement, the following terms shall have the following meanings:
   (a) "Execution Date" shall mean the day upon which the last party to this Agreement shall duly execute this Agreement;
   (b) "Option Fee" shall mean the total sum of a down payment of _____ percent (___%) of the total purchase price of the Premises plus all closing costs, payable as set forth below;
   (c) "Option Term" shall mean that period of time commencing on the Execution Date and ending on or before _____, 20____;
   (d) "Option Exercise Date" shall mean that date, within the Option Term, upon which the Purchaser shall send its written notice to Seller exercising its Option to Purchase;
   (e) "Closing Date" shall mean the last day of the closing term or such other date during the closing term selected by Purchaser.

2. **GRANT OF OPTION.** For and in consideration of the Option Fee payable to Seller as set forth herein, Seller does hereby grant to Purchaser the exclusive right and Option ("Option") to purchase the premises upon the terms and conditions as set forth herein.

3. **PAYMENT OF OPTION FEE.** Purchaser agrees to pay the Seller a down payment of _____ percent (____%) of the total purchase price of the Premises plus all closing costs upon the Execution Date.

FIGURE 13.2   Option Agreement for Purchase of Real Property

4. **EXERCISE OF OPTION.** Purchaser may exercise its exclusive right to purchase the Premises pursuant to the Option, at any time during the Option Term, by giving written notice thereof to Seller. As provided for above, the date of sending of said notice shall be the Option Exercise Date. In the event the Purchaser does not exercise its exclusive right to purchase the Premises granted by the Option during the Option Term, Seller shall be entitled to retain the Option Fee, and this agreement shall become absolutely null and void and neither party hereto shall have any other liability, obligation or duty herein under or pursuant to this Agreement.

5. **CONTRACT FOR PURCHASE & SALE OF REAL PROPERTY.** In the event that the Purchaser exercises its exclusive Option as provided for in the preceding paragraph, Seller agrees to sell and Purchaser agrees to buy the Premises, and both parties agree to execute a contract for such purchase and sale of the Premises in accordance with the following terms and conditions:

   (a) Purchase Price. The purchase price for the Premises shall be the sum of _____ _____ ($_____); however, Purchaser shall receive a credit toward such purchase price in the amount of the Option Fee thus, Purchaser shall pay to Seller at closing the sum of _____ ($_____);

   (b) Closing Date. The closing date shall be on _____, 20____ or at any other date during the Option Term as may be selected by Purchaser;

   (c) Closing Costs. Purchaser's and Seller's costs of closing the Contract shall be borne by Purchaser and shall be prepaid as a portion of the Option Fee;

   (d) Default by Purchaser; Remedies of Seller. In the event Purchaser, after exercise of the Option, fails to proceed with the closing of the purchase of the Premises pursuant to the terms and provisions as contained herein and/or under the Contract, Seller shall be entitled to retain the Option Fee as liquidated damages and shall have no further recourse against Purchaser;

   (e) Default by Seller; Remedies of Purchaser. In the event Seller fails to close the sale of the Premises pursuant to the terms and provisions of this Agreement and/or under the Contract, Purchaser shall be entitled to either sue for specific performance of the real estate purchase and sale contract or terminate such Contract and sue for money damages.

6. **MISCELLANEOUS.**

   (a) Execution by Both Parties. This Agreement shall not become effective and binding until fully executed by both Purchaser and Seller.

   (b) Notice. All notices, demands and/or consents provided for in this Agreement shall be in writing and shall be delivered to the parties hereto by hand or by United States Mail with postage prepaid. Such notices shall be deemed to have been served on the date mailed, postage prepaid. All such notices and communications shall be addressed to the Seller at _____ and to Purchaser at _____ or at such other address as either may specify to the other in writing.

FIGURE 13.2 (*Continued*)

(c) Fee Governing Law. This Agreement shall be governed by and construed in accordance with the laws of the State of _____.

(d) Successors and Assigns. This Agreement shall apply to, inure to the benefit of and be binding upon and enforceable against the parties hereto and their respective heirs, successors, and or assigns, to the extent as if specified at length throughout this Agreement.

(e) Time. Time is of the essence of this Agreement.

(f) Headings. The headings inserted at the beginning of each paragraph and/or subparagraph are for convenience of reference only and shall not limit or otherwise affect or be used in the construction of any terms or provisions hereof.

(g) Cost of this Agreement. Any cost and/or fees incurred by the Purchaser or Seller in executing this Agreement shall be borne by the respective party incurring such cost and/or fee.

(h) Entire Agreement. This Agreement contains all of the terms, promises, covenants, conditions, and representations made or entered into by or between Seller and Purchaser and supersedes all prior discussions and agreements whether written or oral between Seller and Purchaser with respect to the Option and all other matters contained herein and constitutes the sole and entire agreement between Seller and Purchaser with respect thereto. This Agreement may not be modified or amended unless such amendment is set forth in writing and executed by both Seller and Purchaser with the formalities hereof.

IN WITNESS WHEREOF, the parties hereto have caused this Agreement to be executed under proper authority:

As to Purchaser this _____ day of _____, 20_____ .

Witnesses: "Purchaser" _____

As to Seller this _____ day of _____, 20_____ .

Witnesses: "Seller" _____

FIGURE 13.2   (*Continued*)

"Flex Option Agreement." A flex option allows you to get a property under contract and then put your buyer and seller together. For your service, you receive an option release fee at the closing. It is best used when the seller is also an investor and understands the business. Be sure to check with your local attorney before using an option or flex option. If you would like to download your own option or flex option agreement to edit any way you

Date: _____

Optionor _____ referred to as (SELLER) and
Optionee _____ referred to as (BUYER), has an option to buy the
above listed property for the sum of _____ Dollars ($_____)
under the terms that buyer or seller may stipulate. Option consideration in the amount of TEN
DOLLARS ($10) is hereby acknowledged by both parties.

The Buyer has right to purchase the property within 30 days of date of this contract and
additionally can assign or sell this option to a qualified buyer (New Buyer) meeting all terms
and conditions as required from Seller.

Upon nonperformance of Buyer to exercise this option no remedies cumulative by either
party will be applicable and the option consideration paid by buyer shall be the sole remedy
under this agreement.

If this option is assigned by Buyer to other interested party (New Buyer) meeting the required
terms of Seller then the terms of compensation to Buyer for release of this option agreement
shall be _____ Dollars ($_____).

Providing the name of the New Buyer to the seller shall be sufficient notice to seller for buyer
to receive the option release fee upon closing of the transaction between the seller and new
buyer. The option release fee is to be paid at closing and listed as an option release fee.

Optionor/Seller _____   Date _____

Optionee/Buyer _____   Date _____

Copyright 2009 © by Larry Goins. To customize this document, download Figure 13.3 to your hard
drive from www.realestatedaytrading.com/bonuses. The document can then be opened, edited, and
printed using Microsoft Word or another popular word processing application.

FIGURE 13.3   Flex Option Agreement

want, then you can go to www.RealEstateDayTrading.com/Bonuses. and
click on the forms tab.

Simultaneous Closing

This is like having two closings back to back, with your buyer funding your
purchase. You are closing in your name or your company name, but you
do not have to bring any funds to the closing. Not every attorney or title
company will allow you to do a simultaneous closing. You will just have

to ask your attorney or title company if they do these types of transactions. They will know what you are talking about. You can also ask fellow investors at your investors club meeting or the leaders of the club to refer you to attorneys and title companies that will do simultaneous closings. You will have to pay two sets of closing costs when you do a simultaneous closing.

Many problems that arise in a closing come from this type of transaction. For example, if you do not have your own funds to close and your buyer backs out, then you can't close, your seller will be upset, and they might even resort to suing you for specific performance.

Clause number three that I described in Chapter 9 protects you from this. Remember, clause number 3 states that the deposit shall be the sole remedy in the event of a buyer's default. So always make sure to put clause three in every contract.

You can use the simultaneous close method safely if you have backup buyers in place to jump in and save the deal at the last minute and if you have your own cash or a day funder who will put up the cash at a moment's notice. But if you have the funds, you might as well close the deal the standard way with a physical close, just don't make things too complicated. Make sure that if you have to keep the property for more than a few hours that you get an owner's title policy and a builder's risk insurance policy in the event of damage to the property while you are the owner of record.

Physical Closing

Physical closings are when you actually buy and fund the property either with cash or day funding. This is the most expensive method because you are paying two sets of closing costs just like in a simultaneous closing. With this method you need to have your funding lined up in advance so you can close regardless of what happens to your buyer. Account for the extra cost of two closings in your instant property analysis. That way your maximum allowable price will allow you to collect more than your $5,000 or more fee so that you can pay for the closing and any other costs you incur along the way, such as home inspection, title search, and appraisal fees.

My good friends Ross Treakle and his brother Graham have come up with a service that offers access to many forms that auto fill so that once you have the buyer's or seller's information it will auto fill all of the documents for you. You can check it out at www.InstantFormGenerator.com.

CHAPTER 14

DUPLICATE AND DELEGATE: PUT 92 PERCENT OF THE WORK ON AUTOPILOT AND STREAMLINE THE REST

In the beginning stages of building your business, you should be completely involved in every aspect of the business. You should build the day trading system. Develop your buyers list and your sellers database, prepare your contracts, line up your source of day trading funds, and recruit a dream team of professionals to help you.

Then you can start making offers and doing some deals. At this point, you should delegate as much of the work as possible to others. Automate everything you can. Hire answering services or call capture services to take initial calls from buyers and sellers. Let your services screen out the suspects and give you the prospects to talk to personally. Use bird dogs to bring you deals. Use scouts to drive around your target neighborhoods looking for vacant houses in need of repair.

Automate your follow-ups using autoresponders to contact and keep in touch with buyers, sellers, realtors, and professionals on your dream team. Delegate your closings to your attorney or title company. You sign off on every deal. But once you sign off on it, let your professionals handle the documents and formalities of closing. This allows you to spend your time doing what is most important to your business: making offers.

By now, you should be closing lots of deals and have your day trading business up and running. But you are still involved. You are still an important part of making offers and buying and selling houses. I personally never do this anymore. I don't do any prospecting, networking, or marketing to find motivated buyers and sellers. I don't deal with contractors, appraisers, title companies, or home inspections. I don't get involved in closings.

I don't search for professionals to help close my deals. I don't even make offers. And I'm not involved in negotiations with sellers. I don't advertise for buyers. Yet I sell about 10 houses a month and receive a steady cash income. I'm not involved in the day-to-day business because I learned how to duplicate myself. I didn't go into real estate to replace my job. I didn't quit one job just to get another job. I want to be free and independently wealthy. I've done this by duplicating myself.

DUPLICATE YOURSELF

There are two ways to duplicate yourself: Hire virtual assistants for all the routine and administrative tasks of the business and hire property acquisition managers to make offers, negotiate deals, and buy and sell houses for you.

You can hire virtual assistants to do the things that you are currently doing, like scanning the Internet for motivated sellers who own distressed houses. Virtual assistants can track down contractors, title companies, home inspectors and appraisers in the areas where you want to buy houses. And remember, it doesn't have to be where you live. Using this day trading system, you can buy and sell houses that are located in the next state or clear across the country. We have day traded houses in nine different states so far. There is no geographical limit to day trading houses.

Hire Virtual Assistants

Many businesses are using virtual assistants. A virtual assistant is someone who does tasks for you but does not work from your location. It could be a secretary, salesperson, graphics designer, telemarketer, or so on. The neat thing about using virtual assistants is that you do not need an office location for them to go to. There are many web sites you can use to hire them. Some web sites list the people looking for work, their skills, and candidates may even have taken tests at the web site and been graded on their skills in certain areas.

For example, if you go to www.odesk.com you can search for a virtual assistant in the Philippines that offers customer service or telemarketing skills and will work for between $1 and $3 per hour. Then you hire the virtual assistant to take calls from people who need to sell their houses. Just give your virtual assistant a script, and they can separate the suspects from the prospects for you. Then you are not wasting your time. Think about it. For only $40 to $120 a week you can have a full-time person taking all of your calls.

If you do not have that many leads coming in yet, your virtual assistant could also do other things for you like signing you up at Yahoo! groups, creating profiles on some of the social networking sites, making calls on the for sale ads on the Internet to find properties, helping you build your buyers list, and more.

The reason you want to choose virtual assistants from the Philippines is that they speak very clear English and have great work ethics, not to mention the fact that they will work for you very inexpensively. However, if you find one that you like, I would suggest that you pay them a little more than they are requiring to keep them happy and from looking for another job.

Virtual assistants can help you with any routine or random tasks that don't require your physical presence. I've listed some of the tasks that virtual assistants can do for you:

- *Web and Internet assistance:* Web site design, logo design, Internet marketing, Google and Yahoo! PPC advertising, get traffic to your web site, Web 2.0 online marketing, find new buyers and sellers for your database, post to online classified listing sites, search online classified listing sites, add an online chat to your web site, sell stuff for you on eBay, create new social networking accounts and profiles, manage your social media accounts, or extend your social networking presence.
- *Routine e-mail, fax, and phone assistance:* Handle routine e-mails, faxes, and phone calls using the guidelines you provide; forward out of the ordinary e-mails; route fax and phone messages to you; routine follow up with new clients; screen out distractions and nonessential busy-work so that you can concentrate on making offers and negotiating deals; take a stack of business cards and input them into your database.
- *Administrative assistance:* Help your buyers/investors make offers on houses; answer questions from sellers who want to submit houses for you to buy; manage the freelance scouts who find vacant houses for you; get estimates from contractors; deal with appraisers, home inspectors, and title companies; manage closings by keeping all parties,

lenders, attorneys, title company, realtors, and others apprised of schedules and providing them with needed documentation.

Here are some great sites that offer virtual assistants so you can delegate everything you would ever need to do in your day trading business: TasksEveryday.com, elance.com, longerdays.com, HireMyMom.com, VA4U.com, and hirevirtualassistants.com.

HIRE IN-HOUSE PROPERTY ACQUISITION MANAGERS

This section is very exciting because it tells you how I was able to go to the next level and take myself completely out of the day trading process. I'll teach you how to automate yourself right out of a job, like I did. What would you do if you didn't have to work? Michael Gerber would be proud!

Think about it: You could sleep as late as you want; spend more time with friends or family; spend your days fishing, trekking through the Appalachians, or sailing the Caribbean, while the money keeps coming in automatically. Now I have time to help raise my son and daughter, and spend afternoons and evenings with my wife at our new lake home. I just got back from a two-week Alaskan cruise. Did my company suffer without me? Not a bit. They hardly knew I was gone. I'm reachable in case of an emergency, but for day-to-day business, I'm absolutely not needed.

It's all possible because I was able to hire independent property acquisition managers to buy and sell houses for me. I have more time, and I can day trade many more houses. If I am the only one identifying houses, making offers, contracting, and buying and selling houses, then there are only a certain number of houses that I can buy. By duplicating myself with three additional people, I can day trade three times as many houses.

How did I get to this point? I hired independent property acquisition managers to follow the instructions and do the deals just like I did them before.

Make sure you personally know all of the processes and procedures of buying and selling property before trying to hire someone to work for you. The worst thing that could happen is that the person you hire knows more than you about closing. Also, no matter how successful you become and no matter how many people you hire, it is very important that you continue to sign off on any upcoming closings.

Property Acquisition Managers: Commission-Based Employees

Each property acquisition manager is a commission-based employee of my company. I give them the opportunity to earn commissions on their own deals and on the deals of trainees who work under them.

Everyone starts as apprentice. An apprentice uses my real estate day trading system to buy and sell properties and train apprentices under them as well according to the guidelines provided. They are taught the same things that you have learned in this book. New employees have 90 days to close their first transaction.

The commission pay rate is based on the net amount of income each apprentice generates for the company. On income from $0 to $10,000, the apprentice gets 15 percent commission; from $10,001 to $25,000, the commission is 20 percent; and on income in excess of $25,001, the commission is 25 percent.

When they start, each apprentice is assigned a team leader. The team leader gets paid the exact same thing as the apprentice when they close a deal. This means that the team leader has a vested interest in helping the apprentices close their deals. If an apprentice closes a deal and makes $2,500, then their team leader also gets paid $2,500 just for being there to help.

After an apprentice closes five deals, he or she may become a team leader. After an apprentice becomes a team leader, the person who was his or her team leader will still make 10 percent of what the new team leader makes on personal transactions and on their apprentice's transactions.

All apprentices and team leaders have the goal of making a minimum of 10 offers a day. And they also have the goal of putting properties under contract according to the following schedule:

30 days: One property under contract.
60 days: Three under contract and one closing.
90 days: Five under contract and two closings.

Hiring Property Acquisition Managers

When hiring someone, please make sure that you know all of your state's rules, regulations, and requirements for hiring and paying employees. This includes reporting and paying taxes as well. If you are thinking about hiring people as independent contractors, just make sure that you know the laws and the IRS rules and test for determining whether or not a person is considered an employee or an independent contractor. The IRS has a 20-rule test, which you can find at www.IRS.gov.

The most important thing that I can stress to you when hiring people to work in your day trading business is to find honest, ethical, and moral people, with a good work ethic. They don't have to have any real estate experience. In fact I would rather that they didn't.

The best way to deal with this up front is to have a conversation about the bigger picture. Everyone has plans, goals, and dreams. They just don't know how to go about achieving them. A job with your company could be the opening that will enable your employees to achieve something important in their lives.

I have a great team in my office, and they work very hard and make a lot of money buying and selling houses with me.

Managing Property Acquisition Managers

You want to hire people to help you. But you need to maintain control. You've got to stay involved in the business, oversee your employees, and sign off on everything. It's like my mother-in-law Lynn says, "The best fertilizer in an orange grove is the footsteps of the owner." I have never forgotten that and never will. Make sure you are the fertilizer for your organization.

CHAPTER 15

QUICK START YOUR
$5,000 TO $10,000 DAY
TRADING PAYDAYS

Congratulations. You've gotten this far. You're almost done. By now, you have absorbed a lot of information about real estate day trading. And now you know more than many veteran investors know. You have a huge advantage that will enable you to buy and sell houses in one day like I do 5 to 10 times every month.

NOW WHAT DO YOU DO?

Read this book again. Learn what's in these pages, so that when you start your day trading business you can refer back to this book frequently to find out what to do every step of the way. I'm going to summarize the whole process for you in this chapter.

But before I do, I want to stress one important thing: education. It was education that taught me what I needed to know to create my unique day trading system. I'm not talking about a Harvard MBA or a Wharton Business School kind of education. I'm talking about learning real-world knowledge of the real estate day trading business.

After all, I do not have a college degree. I'm not knocking people who have one. I just didn't have the money or the grades to get into college. I just want to make sure that you do not confuse having a college degree with making money. Sure, if you have a degree you can get a good paying job and maybe even be in management, but I am sure that you know or have known someone whose job was downsized. The only job security you have in today's marketplace is in your ability to make money!

I almost forgot, even though I don't have a college education, I do have a South Carolina PhD... That's a Public High School Diploma. I can say that because I live in South Carolina!

FOUR-STEP QUICK-START CHECKLIST

Remember, real estate day trading is a systematic way to buy and sell houses in one day. But you aren't going to put this book down and just start day trading houses. It doesn't work that way. I know you have been through a lot of information and are probably wondering, "Where do I start?" I wanted to give you a quick rundown of what you need to do in order to get started. Here is a short list of what you need to do to get started in the order you need to do them:

1. Learn how to analyze a deal so you can start making offers.
2. Line up your funding so you can make all-cash offers.
3. Build your buyers list to have someone to sell your properties to fast.
4. Start making offers.

ADVANCED DAY TRADING EDUCATION—YOURS FREE

So that you can dramatically increase your understanding of the real estate day trading business, I want you to be my guest at my Advanced Real Estate Day Trading Three-Day Boot Camp! In three days, my team and I will teach you the day trading system to help you get started. I urge you to attend. It is a fabulous weekend that will change your life forever. And best of all, it's absolutely *free* with my compliments, for simply buying this book. It normally costs $2,500 and takes place about eight times a year. We will provide you with all of the details about how to sign up for one of these events. When you leave on the last day, you'll be a true master, able to wheel and deal like the best of us. For more details simply go to www.realestatedaytrading.com.

And best of all, you are invited to book a free Day Trading Strategy Session with one of my team members. My strategy sessions are awesome. In these one-on-one sessions over the phone, we go over your strengths and weaknesses to help you jump-start your real estate day trading business. To book your free strategy session as an owner of this book, go to www.RealEstateDayTrading.com and click on free strategy session.

I hope you have enjoyed *Getting Started in Real Estate Day Trading*.

INDEX